PENGUIN BOOKS

ROLLING THUNDER LOGBOOK

Born in Illinois in 1943, Sam Shepard grew up in California, came to New York City as an actor in 1963, and began writing that same year. His first plays, *Cowboys* and *Rock Garden*, were produced as a double bill in 1964. Extremely prolific, he has since then written many provocative (and often award-winning) dramas, among them *La Turista, Forensic and the Navigators, Operation Sidewinder, Back Bog Beast Bait,* and *The Tooth of Crime*. His work has been staged in various American cities as well as in London and has been translated and performed, in theaters and on radio, in France, Germany, Belgium, Holland, Yugoslavia, and other countries. Reviewing his most recent play, *Angel City*, the critic Martin Gottfried wrote: "Once again he is exploring the landscape of an American mythology he seems more aware of than any other contemporary playwright. . . . It is he who is the pure artist, he the prophet of technological mysticism, he, surely, the most influential young playwright in America."

Also by Sam Shepard

PLAYS
Five Plays
La Turista
The Unseen Hand and Other Plays
Operation Sidewinder and Other Plays
The Tooth of Crime
The Curse of the Starving Class and Other Plays

SHORT STORIES
Hawk Moon

ROLLING THUNDER LOGBOOK

By

SAM SHEPARD

Penguin Books

Penguin Books Ltd, Harmondsworth,
Middlesex, England
Penguin Books, 625 Madison Avenue,
New York, New York 10022, U.S.A.
Penguin Books Australia Ltd, Ringwood,
Victoria, Australia
Penguin Books Canada Limited, 2801 John Street,
Markham, Ontario, Canada L3R 1B4
Penguin Books (N.Z.) Ltd, 182–190 Wairau Road,
Auckland 10, New Zealand

First published in the United States of America
by The Viking Press (A Richard Seaver Book) 1977
Published in Penguin Books 1978

LIBRARY OF CONGRESS CATALOGING IN PUBLICATION DATA
Shepard, Sam, 1943–
Rolling Thunder logbook.
1. Rolling Thunder Revue (Musical group)
2. Dylan, Bob, 1941–   I. Title.
[ML3561.R62S55   1978]   784'.06'573   77-11648
ISBN 0 14 00.4750 6

Printed in the United States of America by
Halliday Lithograph Corporation, West Hanover, Massachusetts
Set in VIP Times Roman

ACKNOWLEDGMENTS

Big Sky Music: lyrics on page vii from "When I Paint My Masterpiece" by Bob Dylan, copyright © Big Sky Music, 1971, 1976; used by permission; all rights reserved.

Lion Publishing Co., Inc.: lyrics on page 52 from "Never Let Me Go" by Joseph Scott, copyright © Lion Publishing Co., Inc., a division of ABC/Dunhill Music, Inc., 1954; used by permission only; all rights reserved.

Ram's Horn Music: lyrics on page 53 from "Oh, Sister" by Bob Dylan and Jacques Levy, copyright © Ram's Horn Music, 1975, 1976; used by permission; all rights reserved.

Allen Ginsberg: poem on page 38, "Lay down yr Mountain."

All photographs are by Ken Regan/Camera 5 except for the following:
Boston Convention and Tourist Bureau, pp. 133, 143; John Dark, p. 3; Terry Deming, p. 65; copyright © Elsa Dorfman, 1977, pp. 73, 148, 149, 173; Lake Champlain Chamber of Commerce, Burlington, Vermont, Photo by Conant, p. 127; Mayotte Magnus, p. 130; Niagara Falls, New York, Chamber of Commerce, p. 120; Newport, Rhode Island, Chamber of Commerce, p. 102; NYT Pictures: Robert M. Klein, p. 12, Larry Morris, p. 168; Plymouth, Massachusetts, Chamber of Commerce, pp. 25, 41; Alain Resnais/New Yorker Films, pp. 44, 45, 106, 107; The United Society of Shakers, p. 159; Wide World Photos, Inc., pp. 2, 5, 7.

This book is dedicated to
"B-Unit" Camera Crew:

     Dave Myers
     Larry Johnson
     Tom Stearn
     George Stephanson

and to Rudy Wurlitzer—who helped me
over the first hump of this thing

I left the road
And I was seein' double

But it sure has been
One helluva ride.
                    B.D.

Rolling Thunder Revue.

Introduction

This book has taken on such a fractured form not for the sake of "art" or experimentation but rather because the form is a direct outcome of a fractured memory. I was originally hired as a writer to work on a proposed film with the Rolling Thunder Revue, but that role very quickly dissolved into the background and was replaced by a much more valuable situation. I found myself in the midst of all these traveling people as a collaborator in a whirlpool of images and shifting ideas. All of us working together for the same purpose—to try to live in constant movement on the road for six weeks, traveling by land, putting on music, filming this music in the surroundings of broken American history in small New England towns in the dead of winter. Whatever the reasons were behind this reason doesn't seem to matter. All that matters is that it happened. The purpose of this book isn't to reveal a plodding blow-by-blow account of the sequence of events or to play peekaboo with the private lives of the stars but just to give the reader a taste of the whole experience. If that happens, the book is alive.

California

Johnny Dark is behind the wheel. The white Chevy Nova is rolling down through San Anselmo, lazy, spoiled brat of a California town. Teen-age pool halls, sporting goods, Arco stations. The rear end of the car is dragging from the weight of roofing paper and galvanized nails.

"It's hard to see Dylan ever hitting what he once was back in the sixties," pipes up Johnny out of nowhere. "I mean I guess it's not in the cards or something. He already had his day, I guess." I'm daydreaming on the three-year lease we've just landed on a twenty-acre horse ranch and thinking about all the work that's left to do before we can move in. We've got less than a week left to get it all done and the idea of Dylan seems like a distant ghost. It's a long way back to the mid-sixties and dancing naked to "How does it feel?" in the bedroom of an older woman.

"I mean he still writes some good songs, but it's not like it was back then. I couldn't believe it the first time I saw 'Everybody Must Get Stoned' on the juke box. I mean there it was on the juke box, right in front of everybody. Right there in a restaurant on Christopher Street. I couldn't believe you could play that kinda stuff in public while you were eatin' your cheeseburger." Johnny keeps shifting the gears and

Dylan in the sixties.

talking to the windshield. I'm filled with a mixture of the past and all this new life happening to me now. Installing wood-burning stoves, roofing, fencing, foaling corrals, getting ready for the rains.

We slide off the freeway at the Paradise Drive exit, past Big 4 Rents, Denny's, North Bay Lumber Company. He's still going on about the life expectancy of a star and how "even events have a birth, life, and death." We pull up in the suburbs. Temporary digs. An area that looks like the outcome of a recent battle between opposing bands of landscape architects, having nothing to do with the original lay of the land. Inside, on a pine table, is a green note: "Dylan called— Will call back later." I'm standing there staring at it, surrounded on all sides by cardboard Safeway boxes filled with books, toys, everything collected for the big move. "Dylan called?" I can't put it together. Something won't compute.

"We were just talking about him," shouts Johnny over a stream of piss from the bathroom.

"Dylan called here? Why would Dylan call? I don't even know him." I'm weaving sideways through the kitchen repeating the note out loud. My eyes finally fall on an L.A. phone number at the bottom of the note. I return the call but no Dylan. Instead, I get an entangled series of secretaries, lawyers, business managers, each one with a guarded approach.

"Shepard? Shepard who? Are you the one who killed his wife?"

"No, I'm the astronaut."

"Oh. Well, what's all this about? Why did Dylan call you?"

Sam Shepard.

3

"That's what I'm calling you about."

"Oh. Well, just a minute. I'll see if I can find somebody."

The phone goes blank and then a new voice. A man voice. Then blank again. Then a woman voice. Then back to a man.

"Yes, Mr. Shepard. Let me explain. Bob is going on a secret tour in the Northeast. He's calling it Rolling Thunder—the Rolling Thunder Revue."

There's something about the way this chump is calling Dylan "Bob" that immediately pisses me off, combined with the confusion of trying to figure out where in the hell the Northeast is exactly. Before I know it, something hostile is coming out of my mouth.

"If it's so secret, how come you're telling me about it?"

This doesn't go over so good on the other end. A long blankness. I try to soften my inflections as best I can. "Well, what's he want me for? I've got a green note here that says he called."

"Yes, you see, he's doing a movie of the tour and he wants a writer."

Ahaa! Writer! That's me. Writer. "Okay, what's the scoop?" (In my best Chicago-reporter style.)

Then comes a long vagueness about a projected film with me somehow providing dialogue on the spot for all the heavies.

"It's going to be a high-pressure situation. You're used to working under pressure, aren't you?"

"Oh, yeah. Sure. I don't scare easy, if that's what you mean."

"Good. When can you leave?"

That's how it works, right? Dylan calls you and you drop everything. Like the lure of the Sirens or something. Everybody dropping their hoes in mid-furrow and racing off to the Northeast somewhere. I'm bleating into the phone. "This couldn't have come at a worse time. I'm right in the middle of moving into a horse ranch." Zero on the other end. Absolute nothing. The guy must've gone unconscious on the "horse ranch" part. "You still there?"

"So when can you leave?" comes the voice. "Tomorrow?" The pressure's already on and I haven't even packed my toothbrush yet. Half an hour ago everything was cool. I was inside my life. Now it's like a hurricane has struck my intestines.

"Look, I gotta have some time to think about this." My stomach feels like Luca Brozzi has just knocked on the door to collect my debts. "I don't fly either. I only take trains. Haven't flown since Mexico, 1963." Loud, exasperated exhale on the other end as though the guy's convinced he's got a turkey on the line.

"Jesus, that's going to take you a week to get out there then. They're leaving New York at the end of the week. You gotta leave right away." There's a charley horse in my left arm from the grip on the phone.

"All right, all right, I'll let you know first thing in the morning." Phones go down and I'm gasping for air.

"Santa Fe"

The *Santa Fe* is gone. The era of Great Train Competition has been swallowed whole by the government and spit out under the science-fiction handle of Amtrak. Same trains, different colors. Different symbols. No more beautiful orange-and-red Indian chief in flaming feathers, brown hawk-beak nose pointing down the tracks. Now it's a hard-edged blue-and-red-arrow symbol. Straight business. Transportation. Same level as the subways. The government is moving your body from one place to another. No messing around. After all, the Great Plains are just a blank space to get across between East and West. Who wants to feel like they're actually traveling across land. Once you're inside it feels the same though. Same spasm rocking motion. Same forty-year-old cars. Quick change of balance in the body so you don't go sailing into somebody's dinner. Staggering down through narrow aisles. Falling through curtained bedroom compartments. Best place to hear the tracks is when the toilet flushes and that stained aluminum pan at the bottom opens up and yawns at the bare earth.

Now I'm really on it. The Iron Horse heading East. Sacramento, Cheyenne, Chicago. I used to think the only place to write was on a train. Perfect temporary environment. On the road to see the "Wizard."

Chicago Connection

The Chicago connection's made. I'm rolling again. This time the bed is placed horizontal to the train and makes for total insomnia. Black window. The union porters are all black again but this time infected with that familiar New York cynicism. The whole feeling on this train is New York. It's like a testing ground before you strike Manhattan. Just to see if you can take it. I take it lying down. I lock myself in. I go out to eat and that's it. I'm seated in the dining car with a black kid from Baltimore. Shades, floppy hat, wild paranoid eyeballs, long fingers. He talks like a seasoned train rider. "I'm gonna bring back my lady from Japan. I married her over there and I'm gonna bring her back and give her a train ride for a present. I'm gonna put her on this train here." He whips out a color snapshot of his white bride and lays it down on top of the silverware, grinning at me all the time. Then he swings into chick stories. Big City chick stories. The kind only a black kid could tell. "Knew this lady, man, she'd eat you alive. I swear to God, man, she'd tore your ass apart. She got herself in trouble, see. She run her number down and got herself knocked up every way but sideways by some dude. Then she had the kid, see. The dude, he split, but she chase him down and git married to the cat, you dig. She force him to it. Then she come back to Baltimore. He stayed down South somewhere and she come back up. And the dude's gettin' some kinda government check, see, and he send some of it up to her to help out with the kid, dig. So she's collectin' this mean green for a time, but then she finds out that if he's outa the picture, she get the whole trip. Can you dig it? So she get her girls together and send them down there and they off the cat. Just murder his ass like that. Then she collect the whole trip. Murder him just to get that check! I'm tellin' ya, man, chicks in Baltimore kill your ass for a nickel. No lie. They mean, man. She a young chick too. Maybe sixteen years old." I don't react. My stomach takes it in along with the crusty cheeseburger. He turns his face toward the window and peers out at Ohio. Vast cold fields. A crust of frost on the harvested corn stumps. He shakes his head at the window. "Man, I'd hate to be stuck out there." I slide back to my room and stand in the middle of it, swinging with the train.

Grand Central

Grand Central finally comes by way of a long greasy tunnel. Like a mine shaft. The men who work the rails even wear lights on their helmets, same as the miners in Pennsylvania. For some reason I just stay sitting in my compartment staring out. Even when the train's fully stopped and people are crashing their luggage down the aisles outside. I can't believe myself here again. This is a far cry from a horse ranch on the side of a mountain in northern California. I move like a zombie toward the door, out into the aisle, down the steel steps onto hard cement. Blue railroad steam. Human movement in all directions. Is this where someone's going to come up to me and introduce himself and lead me down and lead me out and drive me off? And he does. And the whole rhythm of Rolling Thunder starts up like a turbojet on the runway. From the second I hit the pavement.

Lou Kemp

A fisherman by trade. Runs a full-time salmon cannery operation in Alaska when he's not maneuvering through the rock 'n' roll industry. One of Dylan's childhood friends from Minnesota who's been called in to oversee the running of Rolling Thunder. Has a remarkable gift for being able to speak words without moving his mouth. Has Edgar Bergen beat hands down. Lou is the first "heavy" I'm introduced to. In fact I find myself standing in his hotel room, brown shades pulled, midday sun creeping through. Lou is just waking up. His phone has rung six times as he stiff-arms the air looking for the receiver. Surrounding his bed are piles of suede coats, leather bags, T-shirts, assorted laundry, and ice buckets. He buries the phone in his neck while simultaneously zipping his fly. Evidently, last night in the midst of Gerty's Folk City homecoming atmosphere he managed to buy a 1934 Packard coupé, and now he's trying to wrap up the loose ends. "No, I told him I want to keep the Jersey plates. Yeah. Keep the New Jersey plates on the thing. I don't wanna have to buy new licenses. Yeah. They won't be able to trace the parking tickets that way. No, I want it put in a garage. I'm not takin' it on the tour. Look, you just get the insurance on the thing and stick it in a garage. All right? Good." He hangs up. He's breathing heavily, I guess still recovering from a rough night. "Sam, you missed it last night. We got some great stuff on film. Bette Midler was terrific. What do you think of her?"

"I never heard her sing."

"Well, she's terrific. I was thinkin' of asking her to come on the tour. What do you think?"

"I don't know."

"Well, look, you know what you should do? You should go uptown and take a look at the footage we've got. Just take a look at it, and then we can talk some more. Have you met Bob yet?"

"No."

"Well, you will. He's kinda busy now, but he'll tell you all about the film. He's got his own ideas about it."

Raven

Raven enters the room while Kemp wrestles with a T-shirt. Raven's a short, dark Indian-looking kid with heavily muscled arms and a short thick neck. His eyes flash around the room, taking everything in. He holds a briefcase and a stack of papers. Turns out this is the guy Kemp was just talking to on the phone about the Packard. He must've been down the hall in the next room. This is the first shot I get of the telephone mania that seems to grip everyone as soon as a hotel is reached. In the middle of talking to someone, with the distinct impression that you're communicating, he'll reach for the phone in mid-sentence and call somebody. Anybody. Still keeping up the conversation. Or else cars will be stopped in the middle of the turnpike and someone will rush for a phone booth as though his mother has just died.

Raven spreads out all the papers to the Packard on the bed. It's obvious he's held this position of "taking care of business" before. He knows all the moves. He doesn't rattle. He just takes all the orders from Kemp and immediately shifts into gear. The papers are swept up into the briefcase, and he shoots out the door again. Lou is brushing his hair.

Lou Kemp: "One of Dylan's childhood friends from Minnesota."

Up in Midtown

U p in midtown, nighttime, we're walking through glass doors, past security guards who don't look like security guards, more like college-football-fraternity types, into looming cavernous freight elevators with a hundred buttons, down into basements, through padded corridors, then suddenly wall-to-wall yellow carpeting and a black iron gate with one of those black-box electric buzzers on it. The kind of gate you'd find at the driveway entrance to a senator's estate in Virginia. More security on the other side of the gate, checking I.D., passes, who's who, muffled sounds of music coming from somewhere even more secret than this. We're let into it, gate closing behind us with electric click, the underground caves of the White House now, through double-paneled soundproof door, strong sweet smell of Indian incense, Allen Ginsberg making notes in a big blue notebook, looking like Merlin the Magician, people crawling around with coffee in one hand, some people looking like any second they're going to be asked to leave. Bowl of fruit on table, a full band working out on stage. A band that visually looks like exactly what it is—a collection, each member looking like a whole band could be built around him. I sit and watch from floor level. I'm feeling like "this is it," but I don't know what "it" is yet. Bobby Neuwirth greets me from all the way back in the sixties. Instant memory flash of Bobby pouring hot coffee in the lap of a junior Mafioso at Max's Kansas City. (What great karma backlash if it had turned out to be Joey Gallo. But it wasn't.) Ginsberg can't remember where we met or when. It's embarrassing trying to remind him. I had worked on a film called *Me and My Brother* with Robert Frank, and Allen had helped us with research material on Peter Orlovsky's brother, Julius, whom the booby specialists labeled "clinically catatonic." It all comes back to Allen now. The unfolding of Julius's private mind. His lostness in New Jersey. His wanderings barefoot on the Verrazano Bridge. Raised in chicken coops. Burned through the skull by every "modern" form of electric, drug, and psychological coercion. But that was way back then, and even though the pre-media hype is that Rolling Thunder is a return to the sixties, that's not the way it feels right now. Right now, there's music pouring out on us. A band of aces right here in the present. Joan Baez doing a pre-bop boogaloo in front of it all. She's incredible to watch. I never used to think of her as sexy before, but she's definitely that. No more folksy peace-licking Scottish-folk-ballad stuff. She's transformed into a short-cropped shit-kicking Mexican disco dancer. The band is moving into satirical R 'n' B licks, expressing their chops in all directions, people wandering in and out,

"Bobby Neuwirth greets me from all the way back in the sixties."

Ronee Blakely shows up in a black beret and what looks like a black portfolio big enough to house a small piano. Someone asks if I want to meet Dylan, so I follow. Out into the halls again, past dark Coke machines, into a back room, and there he is, lying horizontally across a metal folding chair like he's practicing a levitation trick, both ragged cowboy boots propped up on a metal desk. He's blue. That's the first thing that strikes me. He's all blue from the eyes clear down through his clothes. First thing he says to me, "We don't have to make any connections." At first I'm not sure if he's talking about us personally or the movie. "None of this has to connect. In fact, it's better if it doesn't connect." I start nodding agreement as though I'm too cool not to understand, sliding in something half-baked about "surrealism." I stare at him. He stares back. I realize in a swift flash the unfairness of

"Joan Baez doing a pre-bop boogaloo."

"Ronee Blakely shows up in a black beret."

the situation. He's known through his photographs to anyone who meets him. But faced with him in the flesh, I have a hard time shaking loose of the photographs and just seeing him. All I'm seeing are album covers for about six minutes straight. Then slowly he comes into focus. Behind him, with a telephone jammed in his mouth, Jacques Levy, who co-authored the "Hurricane Carter" song, is in a heated discussion with a lawyer about the libel possibilities of some of the lyrics. He's reworking the lyrics on the phone, trying to come to an agreement. The "Hurricane" single is due to come out in less than a week, and the possibility of a libel suit has everybody on edge, except Dylan. He sips coffee and tips his gray gaucho hat forward on his head.

"Did you ever see *Children of Paradise*?" he says. I admit I have but a long time ago. I saw it with a girl who cried all the way through so it's hard to relate my exact impressions. "How about *Shoot the Piano Player*?"

"Yeah, I saw that one too. Is that the kind of movie you want to make?"

"Something like that." He turns away and nods his foot. This is the first time I get a real taste of his gift for silence. Of feeling no need to fill in the gaps. Of leaving words just hanging in air so that you hear them played back to you in your head. I tell him we're thinking of shooting some footage with Ramblin' Jack, in the bathroom of the hotel. He lights up for a second.

"I gotta wait till we get outa this city. Right now I just feel like gettin' outa here. Once we're up there on the road we'll be able to get into the film more. I'm just waitin' to get outa here now."

Ramblin' Jack

Jack Elliot has this incredible soft touch with people; you feel right off that you've known him for years and he's just continuing where you left off the last time you saw each other. In my case, I'd never laid eyes on him before, not even on stage, so his personableness was really surprising. Right off we were sailing into truck legends, barreling down the narrow northern California logging roads, with him driving on the left-hand side because "that's the way it's done up there." "Loggin' roads are for loggin' trucks, and cars don't have no right a way." He tells me he's been saving up for a brand new Peterbilt truck that he figures to live in for the rest of his life. His technical knowledge of trucks is awe inspiring. Pecos Bill comes flashing back to me. Small-kid cowboy legend, swimming in his tall white hat, black-and-white pony-hide chaps, burbling cactus legends, coyote prairie songs, sailing sky high off the back of every buckin' horse. A wandering, mythical, true American minstrel. Jack keeps ramblin' on to quarter-horse stories, diesel trucks through South Dakota snowstorms. He transforms the hotel room with American landscapes while the film crew is busy packing up its gear. For Jack there's never a better time than the present for wheeling full tilt into any old legend. Makes no difference what's happening in the immediate environment; the only thing that counts is a story, and even better, an exchange of stories. I've had lots of experience being the audience to fired-up speed freaks on the Lower East Side. Listening to their mind-benders while all the time wanting to escape. With Jack it's different though. He's not selfish in that way of nailing your attention down with insane raps. His pleasure is wandering casually in the imagination and just bringing someone else along for the ride. We're heading for the elevator in the Gramercy Park, and I'm wondering about cowboys. About the state of cowboys. About "real life" and "fantasy." About making yourself up from everything that's ever touched you. From Pecos Bill to the Rolling Thunder Revue.

Blasted

8th Street, New York

Phil Ochs is blasted out of his mind and trying to reconstruct the entire plot line of the film *Hard Times* to Dylan, who seems on the verge of taking a swan dive off a balcony in an 8th Street apartment. The apartment is one of those suave, party-oriented jobs with blond people draped all over the furniture. David Blue is handing out animal tranquilizers indiscriminately, in his double-breasted pinstripe gangster suit. Physically he seems like the only dude who could actually handle Phil Ochs if it came down to a matter of meat. Dylan is cranked up on some kind of funny chemical and keeps tapping his entire body to an inside rhythm. His eyes snake around the room, trying to find an opening. He's cornered by a sixteen-millimeter lens, a boom mike, a short girl who keeps referring to marriage, and various acoustic guitar pickers in the background, pretending he's out of earshot. Below, another scene is being set up for the film involving T-Bone Burnett disguised as a professional golfer, complete with golf bag and cap. The place is exploding with crazies. Outside, Ginsberg is yelling from the pavement, one story below, that he's ready for us to film him reading one of his poems. No one seems to hear. The film crew is raining sweat under the hot lights as more and more people cram into the space. Every once in a while somebody's girl friend catches a glimpse of Dylan and tries to get her boyfriend to look up at the top of the stairs. He's crouched like a bat in black leather jacket and chewing on Red Man tobacco. He hands a chew to one of the girls beside him, who feels obliged to bite into it. She spits the whole thing over the balcony. It just misses the Tom Collins of somebody who doesn't seem to notice. The electric fire in the fireplace is being lit for the background motif. T-Bone is lining up a putt on the Persian carpet. We haven't even left town yet.

A Band of Aces

A Dressing Room Marked "Guam"

T-Bone Burnett: Fort Worth, Texas, seven feet tall, "The Lonesome Guitar Strangler," often appeared on stage disguised as Merlin the Magician. Often roped Roger McGuinn around the neck at the conclusion of Roger's famous song "Chestnut Mare." Was responsible for a mysterious gift of on-the-spot action painting incorporating various backstage multimedia such as: spit beer (Miller High Life), crushed chalk, foaming Pepsi, fresh urine, fresh fruit, cream cheese, whipped cream, dried apricots, whole walnuts, Polaroid negatives (that is, Polaroid snapshots before they turned positive), broken Les Paul Gibsons, and various other ingredients too lengthy to go into. He was also a man of instant hunger. If he wasn't served when the hunger hit him, he would systematically set about demolishing the entire restaurant beginning with the menus and working his way up to the chandeliers. On one occasion he ate an entire table.

Howie Wyeth: Smooth drums. Holy ancient American piano. The mellowest fellow I ever laid eyes on. A slouched wool cap that seemed to be growing onto his head. I never saw him without it. Upside-down Chinese splash cymbal. Black tennis shoes. Enjoyed playing music like nobody's business.

Dave Mansfield: Genius kid. Played everything but the kitchen sink. The one often referred to by Allen Ginsberg as "the boy with the Botticelli face."

Steve Soles: Owns a '52 Ford, which is credentials enough for any man.

Rob Stoner: Machine-gun bass. Like a gangster Gene Vincent. The brains behind the operation. The get-it-together man. Responsible for at least one great song ("Wasted"). Grafted harmonies onto Dylan like a Siamese twin.

Luther Rix: Jazz soul. Meditated before every set. Delicate touch on percussion. Hard-driving congas on "Hurricane." Beautiful wife.

Mick Ronson: English guitar hero. What every mother warns her daughters about. Chief instigator of the "make-up" craze which swept through Rolling Thunder like a brush fire. Da da!

Scarlet Rivera: Mysterious dark lady of the fiddle, with whom I never spoke more than three words, not because I didn't want to but because it never happened. Wore snake make-up and often deviated attention on the stage because of her uncanny sense of rhythm and ability to sustain melody lines while weaving vertically.

Opposite: "T-Bone Burnett:
. . . often disguised as Merlin the Magician."

"Howie Wyeth: Smooth drums."

Dave Mansfield and Steve Soles.

"Rob Stoner: Machine-gun bass."

"Luther Rix: Jazz soul."

"Mick Ronson: English guitar hero."

Red Rent-a-Van

Dylan took off in the middle of the night in his camper, him at the wheel. Rumor has it that the camper was busted into and the color TV ripped off. Our camera crew is making time on the New England Thruway in a cracker-box rent-a-van. The kind with the steering wheel set forward from the front axle so you get the feeling you're driving a diving board. The whole chassis throbs violently whenever we approach 50 mph. George Stephanson, who's driving, has a technique of pushing right on through the 50 mph zone and up into the 70 region. His theory is that if the truck blows up, then we can get a new one. So far the thing's withstanding his throttle foot. In his spare time George pilots glider planes, and he's running off a list of all the potential dangers involved. The van's packed to the gills with film equipment. We're all playing leapfrog over one another and establishing little burrows for ourselves, testing how the spine fits into different recesses in the packing. Connecticut's sliding by to the sound of Randy Newman on tape cassette.

"A-Unit" Camera Crew (don't ask me how they came to decide who was "A" and who was "B") is the first to arrive in Falmouth, with Dylan hot on its heels. Dylan careens into the parking lot and approaches the camera crew. "Did you get any rivers? We're gonna need lots of rivers. And trains. Did you get any trains?"

Opposite: "Mysterious dark lady of the fiddle."

". . . in a cracker-box rent-a-van."

Plymouth, Massachusetts

Plymouth is a donut of a town. The kind of place you aspire to get out of the second you discover you've had the misfortune to have been raised there. Even from the point of view of "historical significance," it sucks. Old women dress up in Pilgrim outfits and stand behind counters in counterfeit buildings disguised to look like the "way it was way back when our forefathers first set foot on this great continent," and sell maps of how to get to all the other boring places of significance. They complain about the "damn Pilgrim hat," little white bonnets that keep slipping down their necks. They don't dare take them off in case the inspectors come around. It's been raining fierce all day long and cold too. Night's come and I wander into the Plymouth Memorial Hall, a big brick block of a building. Inside it's a gymnasium where they have the local boxing matches. Ginsberg's religious, chanting finale has been cut from the show, and he sits with Peter in the front row looking dejectedly up at the stage as the technicians prepare the sound check. Allen's general positive outlook though is a constant wonderment to me. He seems determined to roll with the punches and manages to bounce back every time without bitching or cutting someone apart in the process. I wander right through the hall and out back into the night again. I just keep walking until I hit streets. I'm looking for the center of town, if there is one. Thinking of buying a pair of rain boots. Find myself in a Woolworth's. No boots. A kind of demented-looking black guy is buying some pipe fittings, and I ask him if he knows where a person could locate rain boots in Plymouth. He knows a place and says he'll drive me there, if it hasn't already closed. I'm waiting and asking one of the checkout girls if she's going to the concert tonight. "What concert?" "The one in town here. You know, Bob Dylan, Joan Baez? All those people?" "No, I'm not goin'. Couldn't get tickets. Besides, I don't even know those people."

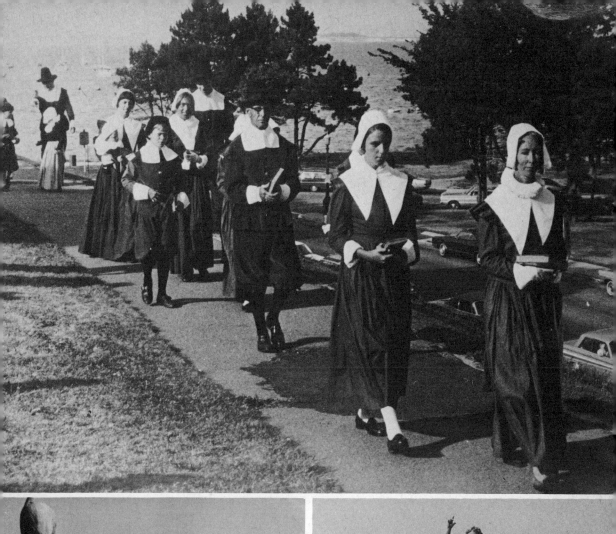

Royce

I find myself in this car with Royce, the black guy who turns out to be a Jehovah's Witness and a plumber on top of that. He's been working all day with his father and says he's too tired to go to any kind of concert. He's heard of Dylan though. Baez too. Used to have a couple of their records. We're driving at night down by the water looking for the rain-boot place, but it turns out to be closed so he hauls me all the way back to the town hall. As we approach it, he begins reminiscing on Jehovah meetings he used to attend in this very town hall as a small kid. He stops the car and we look out at the lines of kids who are gathering outside, huddled up against one another from the cold. "Yeah, we used to have our meetings every Wednesday in there. We had some great meetings." I ask him if he believes in God still and he reassures me he does. Then I ask him if he thinks Dylan believes in God. "Well, I don't know. Some of his poetry sounds like it, but I don't really know if he's a religious person or not. I just couldn't tell ya." I thank him for the lift around town and scoot out.

I'm crossing the wet lawn through the crowds of kids, up the steps, and just as I put my hands on the front door to the place I'm jumped by three meatball types in orange T-shirts with some word printed in black across their chests. "Gotta see some I.D., fella," one of them chortles. I fumble for my pass while the other one starts doing his imitation of Jack Webb frisking a junkie. "Got any cameras? Tape recorders? Anything like that?"

"Nope, not even a TV set. Who are you guys anyway?"

"We're hired by the company."

"What company?" I've never seen them before, but it turns out the promotional outfit from Boston has hired these mugs to harass the kids before they even get inside the hall. They've been standing around for hours in the freezing cold, waiting to get in, only to have themselves and their girl friends pawed all over by a bunch of aspiring narks. Terrific. Finally I make it inside. There's a huge black-and-white slide of Rubin Carter's face projected on the back wall. All the iron railings have been padded with foam rubber and gaffer's tape, as though the authorities were expecting an out-and-out rumble. Backstage, the dressing rooms are actually inside the locker rooms of the gymnasium. In fact the dressing rooms are the locker rooms. Very strange seeing tables full of bright yellow and red roses, fancy chocolates and nuts laid out in a background of Army-green lockers and sweat-stained benches where local boxers have rubbed their jockstraps. The custodian of the hall is in a total blather because Dylan's beagle has shit all over the rug in one of the back rooms. He's

cursing wildly under his breath. "Who in the goddamn hell do these people think they are anyway? Just bring the goddamn dog in here and let him crap all over everything. We never had people like this here before, I'll tell ya that much. We always had well-behaved folks here. Never nothin' like this." He carries the shovel full of dog shit out in front of him like a lantern in the night.

"Kaddish" on the Mah-Jongg Circuit

The Seacrest Hotel, Falmouth, Massachusetts: Hundreds of over-the-top Jewish ladies are firmly entrenched in the hotel before we arrive. They are hellbent on a strange (to a "Mick") Chinese form of dominoes called Mah-Jongg. In fact, it's something comparable to the World Championship Playoffs with money at stake. The fact that superstars are sharing the turf with them is only a side titillation to the ladies. They are obsessed by the game. So imagine their surprise when, late one evening, in the midst of tournament fever, the manager of the hotel announces that there is to be a special poetry reading by "one of America's foremost poets, Mr. Allen Ginsberg!" A warm round of fatty applause. He too is of the same faith after all. Allen approaches the podium, brown suit, papers in hand, looking for all the world like a latter-day Whitman with black trimmings instead of gray. He mounts a tall stool and hunches into the microphone. The ladies smile charitably and Allen begins his piece. His long, terrifying, painful prayer to his mother. These are mothers too, but the needle's too close to the vein. The mothers go from patient acquiescence to giggled embarrassment to downright disgust as Allen keeps rolling away at them. His low rumbling sustained vowel sounds becoming more and more dirgelike and persistent. Dylan sits in the background, back against the wall, hat down over his eyes, listening stilly. Since I was raised a Protestant, there's something in the air here that I can't quite touch, but it feels close to being volcanic. Something of generations, of mothers, of being Jewish, of being raised Jewish, of *Kaddish*, of prayer, of America even, of poets and language, and least of all Dylan, who created in himself a character somehow outside the religion he was born into. Who made a vagabond minstrel in his own skin and now sits facing his very own beginnings. His heritage. And Ginsberg embracing those beginnings so far as to go right through and out the other side into a strange mixture of Eastern mysticism, Hell's Angel meditation, acid, politics, and the music of words. The ladies sit through it. Captured in their own seaside resort. A place they've all come to escape to, and there they are, caught. Allen pounds on. The cameras are weaving in and out of the aisles, creeping up to tables, peering into the matronly faces. Dave Myers, the lead cameraman, is getting a little queasy and

Opposite: " '. . . one of America's foremost poets, Mr. Allen Ginsberg.' "

turned off by the atmosphere. It's not his style to have the emotional content of a scene so obviously contrived. The women wince as the "cancer" stanzas of the epic grind their way toward the finale. Then it ends and there's a surprising burst of applause. Allen thanks them, steps down, and trots off. Joan Baez is introduced and gets a relieved welcome. She does an a cappella "Swing Low, Sweet Chariot" that drives the women wild. Dave Mansfield, the genius kid, steps up with his fiddle, looking like Little Lord Fauntleroy, and impresses everyone with his classical violin technique. His expression never changes. Even when he plays his incomparable slide-guitar riffs with the band, his expression is the same. It's an expression of listening. Intent listening to the inner content of his music. He's an ace musician, for sure. Then comes the blockbuster. Dylan moves up on the platform to the rickety old upright piano used for years for the sole purpose of producing middle-class pablum Big Band sounds of the 30s and 40s. He sits, stabs his bony fingers into the ivory, and begins a pounding version of "Simple Twist of Fate." Here is where it's at. The Master Arsonist. The place is smoking within five minutes. The ladies are jumping and twitching deep within their corsets. The whole piano is shaking and seems on the verge of jumping right off the wooden platforms. Dylan's cowboy heel is driving a hole through the floor. Roger McGuinn appears with guitar, Neuwirth, the whole band joins into it until every molecule of air in the place is bursting. This is Dylan's true magic. Leave aside his lyrical genius for a second and

Opposite: "Joan Baez is introduced."

"Dave Mansfield, the genius kid."

"Dylan's cowboy heel is driving a hole through the floor."

just watch this transformation of energy which he carries. Only a few minutes ago the place was deadly thick with tension and embarrassment, and now he's blown the top right off it. He's infused the room with a high feeling of life-giving excitement. It's not the kind of energy that drives people off the deep end but the kind that brings courage and hope and above all brings life pounding into the foreground. If he can do it here, in the dead of winter, at an off-season seaside resort full of menopause, then it's no wonder he can rock the nation.

Rock 'n' Roll
Heaven

We have an idea that grew from T-Bone and Rob Stoner's obsessions with certain rock 'n' roll heroes of the past. Stoner's favorite is Gene Vincent and T-Bone's is Buddy Holly. We set up a "Rock 'n' Roll Heaven" environment on the veranda of Mel's motel room overlooking a long stretch of beach. Stoner is decked out in full black glitter from head to foot, sitting in an easy chair and having his hair done by Mick Ronson, complete with hair spray and blower. Through the plate-glass window behind him a long girl dressed in a white towel is manicuring her nails. Stoner is concerned about being accepted into Rock 'n' Roll Heaven on the basis of his (Vincent's) latest record. Ronson assures him that everything is in order. "Buddy Holly" enters the scene and is overwhelmed to find "Gene Vincent" there ahead of him, his greatest hero. He sits down to have his ears lowered too. Then enters Ramblin' Jack in the guise of Hank Williams, the gatekeeper to the doors of Rock 'n' Roll Heaven.

Now this is where this film experiment begins to get interesting. We've abandoned the idea of developing a polished screenplay or even a scenario-type shooting script, since it's obvious that these musicians aren't going to be knocking themselves out memorizing lines in their spare time. They're either rehearsing all night, playing a concert, or jamming, and then crashing out about six or seven in the morning. It's almost impossible even to get two or more of them together at the same time in front of the camera. So we've veered onto the idea of improvised scenes around loose situations. What happens in this case is that everyone on the tour has smelled out this scene between T-Bone and Stoner, and one at a time they begin to join into it. Baez suddenly appears in a red wig, hot pants, boots and chewing on a mouthful of gum. She plays a groupie-hooker, hot on the heels of Gene Vincent. Neuwirth falls into it like a dealer carrying a bag full of goodies. He's pouring bottles full of vitamin pills all over the veranda. "I got some chloral hydrates right here for ya. Hank's favorite. Here's a bagful a California Turn-Arounds." Pills are flying all over the place. The whole scene begins to explode and bounce off these different characters until the hand-held cameras can't even cover the territory fast enough. There's too much happening. Elderly couples taking a midmorning stroll on the beach are dazed by the goings-on. People come in from swimming, dripping wet, to take a look. There's no chance of directing the scene or even stopping long enough to make adjustments in camera angles. It's uncorked Marx Brothers stuff. Nothing to do but let it roll and hope there'll be something in the can that looks as good as it feels. Finally everything grinds down and everyone filters off to lunch, leaving trails of multicolored vitamin pills, red wigs, hair blowers stretched out in the sun.

"Stoner is having his hair done by Mick Ronson."

Falmouth, Massachusetts

Every morning Jack Elliot is out running on the beach with a towel draped around his neck, swimming trunks, and sometimes his cowboy hat. He has an even pace. Even in the rain he's running, sometimes straight out into the ocean and falling face down in the freezing Atlantic. He's up early too. His resilience is amazing. Everyone inside eating breakfast is amazed.

Every morning Allen and Peter sit and meditate in their hotel room. I find myself in the room right next door to Ginsberg and wake up to the moaning of Eastern chants and harmonium playing.

Every morning Barry Imhoff, our producer, is eating his strange diet of crisp bacon dipped in mayonnaise.

This is basically a summer resort but we're here in the winter. It's like occupying a ghost town. For a while the only other boarders here were the middle-aged Jewish ladies. Now we're alone. The owner of the place is a huge Peter Ustinov-type fellow with gold rings on his chubby little fingers, a silver medallion hanging by a chain from his neck, and a kind of mincing gait with the belly as the center of gravity. A reporter from *The Village Voice* managed to weasel his way into the hotel this morning and Lou Kemp came up with a brilliant solution. Lock the dude up in a room and put a quarantine sign on the door. Anyone who's interested in jawing with the press can go directly to him without wondering when he's going to jump out at you from behind. I think the guy spent the whole day in there pacing the floor, with no one to talk to.

On the Rock

Bitter cold winds whipping the beach as we try to maneuver a dinghy loaded down with Neuwirth, Ramblin' Jack, Peter Orlovsky, and Dylan at the helm. The whole thing looks like it's jumped right out of that painting of *Washington Crossing the Delaware* except the passengers in this case are all clinging to the side of the boat, shivering from the cold, and looking totally pissed off to be out here in the elements instead of back in the warm hotel. Up on the beach we're trying to figure out a way to get Ginsberg inside the black iron bars that surround Plymouth Rock as though it was thinking of going somewhere illegal. The Rock itself is pathetic. Just the tip of it sticking out of the sand with a bronze plaque, a roof over it to protect it from erosion, I guess, and lines of pedestrians hanging over the railing trying to get a peek at it. The camera crew is racing back and forth between Ginsberg and the Rock and Dylan and the dinghy trying to set up some kind of panning shot. The dinghy is in danger of being swept out to sea by the tides, and it's all we can do to haul the thing up on shore. Ginsberg is already chanting and chiming on a set of Tibetan bells, and the dinghy crew is staggering up the beach toward him. The crowds don't seem to recognize Dylan at all. In fact they don't seem to recognize anything that isn't strapped down and carrying a bronze plaque.

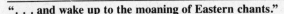

". . . and wake up to the moaning of Eastern chants."

"Lay down yr Mountain"

(written on the tongue)

Lay down   Lay down yr Mountain   Lay down God
Lay down   Lay down yr music   Love Lay down

Lay down   Lay down yr hatred   Lay yrself down
Lay down   Lay down yr Nation   Lay yr foot on the Rock

Lay down yr whole Creation   Lay yr Mind down
Lay down yr Empire   Lay yr whole world down

Lay down   yr soul forever   Lay yr visions down
Lay down   yr bright body   Down yr golden heavy crown

Lay down   yr Magic Hey! Alchemist   Lay it down Clear
Lay down   yr Practice precisely   Lay down your Wisdom dear

Lay down   Lay down yr Camera   Lay down yr Image right
Yea Lay down yr Image   Lay down Light.

Allen Ginsberg
November 1, 1975

Scene for Plymouth Rock

Film

(**W**IZARD [*Ginsberg*] *sitting on Plymouth Rock.* COWBOY [*Ramblin' Jack*] *approaching him as though he'd just come a distance to find this place.*)

COWBOY: Is this here the Kingdom?

WIZARD: This is the Rock.

COWBOY: Oh. You mean this ain't the Kingdom?

WIZARD: This is the Rock in the Kingdom.

COWBOY: Well, where's the Kingdom then?

WIZARD: Good question.

COWBOY: I come all this way just to find it.

WIZARD: Well, they say this is where it started.

COWBOY: But you're not sure if this is it or not?

WIZARD: I have a feeling it might be.

COWBOY: Who are you, if you don't mind my askin'?

WIZARD: I'm the King.

COWBOY: You're the King?

WIZARD: And you're the Cowboy.

COWBOY: That's right! Now, how did you guess that?

WIZARD: How far did you travel?

COWBOY: All the way from the Far West. I traveled all this way just to be here and see it for myself.

WIZARD: Now that you're here, what do you think of it?

COWBOY: Well, it's all right, I guess. A little disappointing.

WIZARD: What were you expecting?

COWBOY: Well, I'd heard that it was undiscovered territory. You know, a new land. Open country. All that kinda stuff.

WIZARD: Well, it is, isn't it?

COWBOY: But you're supposed to be the King.

WIZARD: Yes, I'm the King.

COWBOY: So it's already been discovered then if you're the King.

WIZARD: But we haven't found the Kingdom yet.

COWBOY: Oh, yeah.

Wax Museum

On the ground floor is a full-scale setting of the landing of the *Mayflower*, complete with rocking boat, computerized rainfall, and a tape-recorded narration that responds the second you push a black button on the wall. We've spent hours setting up the lights for a scene with Ginsberg and Jack Elliot. Allen is sitting in the full-lotus meditative pose among several wax Indians who are hiding behind huge wax leaves, peeking out at the white Pilgrims. Jack is inside the actual setting, shaking hands with all the Pilgrims and welcoming them to the new land. He warns them, "Never give your address out to bad company." Then tips his cowboy hat and walks out of the shot. Because of the bad lighting we aren't getting the shot down right, so Jack has to keep repeating this action and saying, "Never give your address out to bad company," over and over again until you wish one of the wax Pilgrims would tell him to shut the fuck up. Jack's begun to liven the scene up somewhat by finding a small platform to jump from and lands square in the back of the small Pilgrim craft, causing the stern to give way. "Looks like you guys'll have to bail out." He starts bailing water with his cowboy hat as the cameraman is yelling to him that he's run out of film. Jack can't hear this piece of information though on account of the computerized rainstorm that cuts in along with the tape-recorded narration. He keeps bailing out with his hat and repeating the phrase "Never give your address out to bad company" over and over again. Allen is waiting patiently in the corner for the cameraman to reload. A whole classful of school kids stampedes down the stairs, herded from behind by two very tight-faced women who turn out to be their teachers. Jack is still bailing from the boat. The kids hit the railing of the display like a flock of gibbons, yelling, "Hey, look, one of 'em's alive! Look, that guy's alive, Mrs. Thornwall!" Mrs. Thornwall is peeling the kids off the railing, sensing right off that things aren't the way they should be at this particular exhibit. Finally the narration-rainfall-ensemble comes to a silent crunch and Jack has a great idea. He breaks out his guitar and sings an old sea chanty to the kids from the midst of the wax dummies. This is truly American History.

Triangle Trade

Film

You wanna hear how we did it way back in those days? We sent us some ships down along to the Indies. Down deep into those sugary islands. Now these little ships were loaded with codfish and cows and some wood from the trees. Now these things were all traded for sugar and molasses and these sugar and molasses were turned into Rum and this Rum was sent way far away to blackest black Africa in return for some slaves and these slaves were sold back to the Indies in exchange for some Gold and this Gold was used to buy goodies from whitest white England. And that's how we did it way back in those days.

Words of a Girl Standing in the Freezing Cold Outside the Red Brick Town Hall in Plymouth, Massachusetts

"**I**'ve never seen him in the flesh. Never seen Dylan. Actually seen him in the same room. So I was curious about this person who I've never seen but who keeps appearing in my dreams. I figure if he keeps appearing like that, in the night, if he keeps coming into my life while I'm asleep, then I should try to actually see him when I'm awake. So I came. I had this one dream where I'm walking down this road in the middle of nowhere. Not surrealistic or anything. Not like a dream but there was this road and I'm walking down it for no special reason and I see Dylan coming toward me. I see him coming and I know it's him even before I see his face. I recognize him somehow and we're coming closer and closer toward each other and then I start jumping up and down in the middle of the road and then he sees me and he starts jumping. We're both jumping like that and not saying anything. Just jumping. And we start jumping higher and higher until we're jumping like fifty feet straight up into the air. Just way up like that then down and back up again. It was real effortless. Real easy and light."

Character References

Alchemist
Magician
Preacher
Poet
Teacher
Medicine Man
Wizard
Saint
Demon
Witch
Gunfighter
Boxer
Prophet
Thief
Cowboy
Devil
Assassin
Bride
Lover
Truck Driver
Pilgrim
King/Emperor
Fisherman
Drifter
Messenger
A Nobody
Priest
Queen
Shaman
Idiot

New England
in General

New England is festering with Bicentennial madness, as though desperately trying to resurrect the past to reassure ourselves that we sprang from somewhere. A feeling that in the past at least there was some form or structure and that our present state of madness could be healed somehow by ghosts. Everywhere replicas of history are being sold. Townspeople are wearing costumes, flags are flying. The present is being swallowed whole by the past. Inside of all this, Rolling Thunder is searching for something too. Trying to make connections. To find some kind of landmarks along the way. It's not just another concert tour but more like a pilgrimage. We're looking for ourselves in everything. Everywhere we stop. Even when we're moving. Trying to locate ourselves on the map. In time and space. The spur behind all this is mainly the film. The hunt for locations, for characters, situations. All these basic ingredients are bringing up questions of who and what we are. What is this whole thing about? Is it a spiritual sojourn of some kind? Just another rock tour? What in the fuck are we doing out here in blind America looking for a hotel room? What kind of film are we making? Just the fact of our being in New England, the land of somebody's forefathers, is having its effect on everything we do. The past is this moment escaping.

Opposite: "New England is festering . . ."

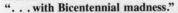

". . . with Bicentennial madness."

Café, Outside Falmouth, Massachusetts

We're being followed by security guards. Our driver, "Big Jack" from the Bronx, has abandoned all pretense of sane driving and seems bent on drilling the fucking accelerator clear through the floorboards. He never lets up, even when we come careening into one of those quaint New England "round abouts" or "traffic circles" or "wheels" or whatever handle they've wound up with. What they are is a direct hangover from the Mother Country, which the Yankees could never cut loose from. In any case, they're dangerous, especially while being negotiated on two wheels at 80 mph. The insanity of the situation only partly dawns on me, because I'm too intent on keeping my body at least touching some part of the seat. Here's this famous singer who for years has had a phobia about being watched and followed and now he's actually being chased by people he's hired or had hired to professionally follow him around. We cut a wide swath of black rubber through the center of what looks like "Our Town," and Jack brings the mighty Plymouth Fury to a panting halt directly across from the local library. No one speaks or moves for about five minutes. We're all numb from the experience except Jack and Dylan, who are out bopping through the golden leaves of fall. The cameraman and his crew are busy cursing and tracking down pieces of equipment scattered throughout the car. A handful of magazine patrons have leaked out of the pharmacy across the street and stand looking across to us as though half expecting a murder or someone to piss in the street. Instead, what happens is that the security car rolls up as slick as a cat, full of fat, grinning security guards all disguised as collegiate meatballs. They park their machine defiantly in the town square and sit there, conspicuously not getting out. Dylan rolls over to them like a miniature bat and sticks his face in the window of the car. He giggles and asks them how come they're following him around. "Barry told us to keep an eye on you." He wheels away from the car and makes a beeline for the inside of the café.

Inside the Café

Inside the café it looks unbelievably like part of another time. Almost to the point of calling it a bad set. There's a narrow counter with a marble top, chrome stools, green malt mixer, aluminum malt glasses, and a high-school soda-jerk kid with thick glasses, a red headband, and a T-shirt. Dylan darts into the men's room and starts growling and making chirping sounds. The soda-jerk kid's never heard of Dylan but says that his older brother has a collection of all his records. After twenty minutes of setting up glaring lights for the sequence, Ernie Eagle starts tapping his fingers on the men's room door and putting his giant ear up to it. After a few tries at this, he tries the door, just in case something's gone wrong. Inside, Dylan is gone, leaving a blowing window framing a pale blue autumn sky.

Alchemist Scene

EMPEROR (*Ginsberg*): I've heard through the grapevine that you have certain powers.

ALCHEMIST (*Dylan*): Oh, that's not me, but I know who you mean.

EMPEROR: You're not the alchemist?

ALCHEMIST: No, but I've seen him come through here carrying his bags full of bottles. We talk now and then.

EMPEROR: What's he tell you?

ALCHEMIST: Nothing special. I've seen him perform certain mysterious gestures though. I never say nothin' about it. I just watch.

EMPEROR: What does he do?

ALCHEMIST: Sometimes very small things and sometimes very big ones.

EMPEROR: Like what?

ALCHEMIST: Well, I've seen him touch fire to ice one time. That was interesting. The whole place melted.

EMPEROR: You were right there?

ALCHEMIST: Right in the middle of it. I stood very still so as not to disturb his activity. Most people ran out of the joint but I stood right there watching.

EMPEROR: What happened then?

ALCHEMIST: Well, next thing I knew we were rolling on ice. But that was some dance he was doing. He showed me other stuff too but I ain't tellin'.

EMPEROR: How come?

ALCHEMIST: 'Cause I want him to come back and show me some more.

EMPEROR: Well, the reason I'm asking is that I'm a little concerned for the Empire.

ALCHEMIST: Why is that?

EMPEROR: Everyone's going bankrupt, and seeing as how I'm the Emperor, I feel it's my duty to bail them out in some way.

ALCHEMIST: Well, I could maybe talk to him for ya. You need gold or lightning?

EMPEROR: Something that's going to pay off the bills.

ALCHEMIST: Well, who do you owe?

EMPEROR: Certain invisible ones. Nobody's sure.

ALCHEMIST: How did you get yourself into this situation?

EMPEROR: I inherited it.

ALCHEMIST: Well, I'll see what I can do for ya, but like I say, I'm not the one.

EMPEROR: I'd certainly appreciate it.

" 'Hurricane' Carter's Bid for New Trial Gets Boost"

TRENTON, N.J. (AP)—Rubin 'Hurricane' Carter's bid for a new trial of his triple murder conviction received a big boost Thursday from the New Jersey Supreme Court, which said it would review the case 'on an accelerated basis.'

"The action bypasses an intermediate appellate court which received the case early this year from Superior Court Judge Samuel A. Larner, who denied Carter and his codefendant, John Artis, a new trial.

"Carter, a former middleweight boxer, says he is innocent of the murders at a Paterson bar in June 1966, for which he and Artis were convicted in 1967.

"Two key prosecution witnesses who had placed Carter and Artis at the scene of the crime have recanted key portions of their testimony."

The New York Times

Carter with Joan Baez.

Trenton jail.

Talk of Poets

L ots a talk of poets flying around. "Improvisers" in the word of Ginsberg. As though the act of flowing wordgrams was a God-given stamp at the moment you come sliding from your mama's thighs. I've seen and heard Neuwirth spin some truly remarkable lines off the top of his cranium, that's for sure. Both sung and talked. Also plenty of stinging sardonicism. Allen too has his own brand of associative arrangements. The list goes on and on but I find it hard to fathom the belief that it's in the blood and not a worked-at process. Seeing as how we're not born with any word language to begin with, there must be a kind of system of thought which a poet gears himself into. Over years. Songwriting is even another story. Even more controlled. As I remember, it was Allen himself who started that riff in the papers about Dylan being the first to bring poetry to the juke box. What did he mean? Excluding Hank Williams? Richard "Rabbit" Brown? Jimmie Rodgers? I guess he meant the sense of poetry expanding consciousness through song or something. I can't figure it out. One thing for sure is that you never doubt it when it hits you. You recognize something going on in your chest cavity that wasn't going on before. When a man can rhyme "kelp" with "help" and cause your heart to lurch—that's poetry. How 'bout the immortal Johnny Ace's C, A-minor, F, G masterpieces which Dylan and Baez do one of in bone-shattering simplicity. Here's just an example of the way it's put together:

> *Just let me love you tonight*
> *Forget about tomorrow*
> *No tears no sorrow*
> *Never let me go.*

Notice the way that even on the boring printed page it takes on an elegant curve and no word is wasted. Better yet, check out the chorus:

> *A million times or more, dear*
> *You said we'd never part*
> *But lately I seem*
> *A stranger in your heart.*

Of course you're missing the amazing descending bass line that traces your emotions right down to the point where the break comes and rejoins the next verse. This isn't meant to be a lesson in lyricism but simply a tribute to Mr. Ace. As far as economy of language goes

" 'Just let me love you tonight.' "

though, Dylan and Levy have really come up with a jewel in "Oh, Sister."

> *Oh, sister, am I not*
> *a brother to you*
> *And one deserving*
> *Of affection*
>
> *And is our purpose*
> *not the same on this earth*
> *To love and follow*
> *His direction.*

Any analysis of lyrics is destined to become as much of a drag as an in-depth discussion of Freudian psychology and belongs to the domain of the critics anyway. My interest is in the inside process, the system of cellular shiftings that goes on as words come sliding from the past into the present. One thing that gets me about Dylan's songs is how they conjure up images, whole scenes that are being played out in full color as you listen. He's an instant filmmaker. Probably not the same scenes occur in the same way to everyone listening to the same song, but I'd like to know if anyone sees the same small, rainy, green park and the same bench and the same yellow light and the same pair of people as I do all coming from "A Simple Twist of Fate." Or the same beach in "Sara" or the same bar in "Hurricane" or the same cabin in "Hollis Brown" or the same window in "It Ain't Me" or the same table and the same ashtray in "Hattie Carroll" or the same valley in "One More Cup of Coffee." How do pictures become words? Or how do words become pictures? And how do they cause you to feel something? That's a miracle.

Sense of Size

Dylan's bought a dog. The size and shape that fit him perfect. Puppy beagle bitch. In heat to boot. Dripping red dots through fancy hotel lobbies from here to Montreal and back. Shits in every corner of a maître d's nightmare. Steals fancy food. Trails Dylan like the hound she is. Gets walks from black security guards, from "Gary the bookie," from "Barry the heavy," from "Louie the fish." She carries a constant hunger and maybe worms even. Once before I saw this capacity of the "Big D" for replicating his physical shape in the outside world. A secret sense of his own size and the visual effect upon all witnesses. The scene is the indoor tennis arena at the Seacrest Hotel in Falmouth, Massachusetts. Strange green-based architecture blazed with giant white Lichtenstein air ducts looming from the ceiling. The entire cavern designed for the tennis addict with money to burn and with health in mind. Rolling Thunder has eaten up the space with gigantic monster black honker speakers, banks of klieg lights, a mammoth yellow canvas backdrop, instruments, amps, microphones, two Super Trooper spotlights mounted from the back like antiaircraft guns, full catering table with all coffee and goodies and stripped cheese and ham and nuts and dried figs, an automatically set Pong machine that doesn't take money, and people crawling around every corner. The stage is set for a "full dress." The tennis arena has been drowned for this moment. The hotel staff has been invited to gawk from metal folding chairs. This will be the first time the show itself has taken shape before an "audience." Neuwirth's miraculous band of street thugs launches into its numbers. No doubt about musicianship. Each one alone could take on an entire decade of rock 'n' roll, country/western, boogie-backstep—you name it. "Accomplished" is too punk for these guys. But then comes Dylan. He appears with a miniature black Gibson, small, catlike, black glasses, white shirt, and Baez beside him, the exact same height, with black hair flashing. They move into "Williams and Zinger" in strange three-four time with the hard accent on the first beat and then building a series of staccato cluster notes around each phrase. The rhythm structure reminds me of the way Red Devil fireworks used to go off when you least expected them to. You lit them and then ran, then came creeping back up on them when they didn't explode. Then just when you were bending down to light the next match they'd all start popping off in a barking chain reaction.

It's this series of props that he's chosen, though, that keeps drilling my attention. From the glasses, to the Gibson, to Baez herself. Everything works in an area of extreme hypnosis. You can't take your

"Dylan's bought a dog."

eyes off the glasses. I had a similar experience watching Ray Charles for the first time, in high school. The crazy sideways, stiff-necked movement of his head and the shades becoming a visual magnet. From the seeing to the blind back to the seeing. The hotel staff take on the postures of film buffs. The only thing missing is the popcorn. They're not sure who or what they're watching. All they're sure of are the names. What appears in front of them is a short, demonic blind man singing strange words ("emptied the ashtrays on a whole other level") with a beautiful Mexican girl. The beagle trots in and out through the coils of microphone wires, oblivious to sound, nose to the ground, hunting for crumbs. Cameras are exploding and the Super Troopers seem on the verge of burning wide holes clear through the canvas backdrop. Ken, the still photographer, lurks on the outskirts like a big-game hunter. It's remarkable how effortless Dylan makes it all seem. He's there in the midst of it, making all this madness coherent just by his presence.

Opposite: "Neuwirth's miraculous band of street thugs."

"But then comes Dylan."

The First Superstar

T-Bone Burnett, a man not given to mincing words, is hovering behind me. He has a peculiar quality of craziness about him. He's the only one on the tour I'm not sure has relative control over his violent dark side. He's not scary, he's just crazy. I'm sitting slouched down in a wicker chair, facing the rehearsal space as Dylan goes through "Hard Rain" like a tornado on the loose. T-Bone keeps pacing behind me making hairpin U-turns in a space of about ten feet. He does a full 180-degree pivot on the heel of his Tony Lama cowboy boots, bends from the waist, and jabs his chin in my neck. I don't move. I'm listening to what he has to say, even though it feels like I'm being mugged on the Lower East Side. His Texas drawl cuts into my ear bones. "I'm so proud of the fucker. The first superstar. He's given me reason to live. I only want to be shot about ten times a day now." He pivots again, then disappears into the dark.

Opposite: T-Bone Burnett.

Roger McGuinn

Roger has a portable telephone that he carries everywhere, contained in a black attaché case, giving him all the aura of a genius gone wrong. He also has a slightly nervous air about him which in certain restaurants, accompanied by his telephone, makes him look like a radical bomber uncertain of his motives. He usually dresses in a black silk top hat, brown hunting jacket, beige jodhpurs, riding boots, and a whip. (The whip is more for show than anything else.) When he appears on stage in this outfit, the audience is in total wonderment as to his true identity until Joan Baez introduces him by name. Then he burns the house down with "Chestnut Mare" or "Eight Miles High" and usually gets roped at the end of it by Burnett and dragged off stage. He explains that it wasn't until the past year or so that he's managed to get over a profound fear of being assassinated on stage. He says that he usually felt the possibility of it coming strongest from the lighting booth in every hall he played in. He'd be singing with the Byrds and all through the song he'd be imagining the hands of the gunman as they polished the barrel with a chamois skin and then the black barrel of the rifle sweeping the width of the stage trying to find the correct angle. Pistols were also within his field of fantasy. One pistol with a silver handle suddenly piercing through the mass of faceless bodies and finding its mark. Sometimes the bullet would find him and he'd go right down, but the crowd would only think that he'd fainted, since they couldn't hear the shot over the sound of the music. Or sometimes the bullet would glance off the guitar and strike some other member of the band. Or sometimes the bullet would miss him altogether. In any case, he's still alive and kicking.

Big Stakes

Astrong recurring feeling I get from watching Dylan perform is the sense of him playing for Big Stakes. He says he's "just a musician," and in his boots he needs that kind of protection from intellectual probes, which are a constant threat to any artist. Even so, the repercussions of his art don't have to be answered by him at all. They fall on us as questions and that's where they belong. Myth is a powerful medium because it talks to the emotions and not the head. It moves us into an area of mystery. Some myths are poisonous to believe in, but others have the capacity for changing something inside us, even if it's only for a minute or two. Dylan creates a mythic atmosphere out of the land around us. The land we walk on every day and never see until someone shows it to us.

Opposite: "He says he's 'just a musician.' "

62

Mama's Dreamaway Lounge

Springfield, Massachusetts, November 7

This was one of the most amazing days on the tour and seemed to come out of pure chance. Through Arlo Guthrie, Ken had contacted an eighty-year-old gypsy lady, known in the vicinity as plain Mama. She ran a small bar/diner-former brothel somewhere out in the extreme boondocks of Massachusetts, a place called Becket. We pulled in on a warm, sunny afternoon after having stopped periodically along the back-country roads to leave little white notes pinned to trees for the buses to follow. "Lay Lady Lay" is softly drifting out of a shack behind a bulging apple tree. Guthrie's funky half-ton Ford is parked in front of the Lounge, a place that immediately gives the impression of eccentricity and oddball taste. There's nothing imposing about it, just a kind of eclectic atmosphere to the trimmings. Inside, every inch of wall space is taken up with ancient photography, mostly images of Mama in various stages of her adventurous life. In some she's posing with a group of chorus girls, guitar strapped to her shoulders, dressed in full gypsy regalia. One of her cheek-to-cheek with a sea captain. Mixed in with the photos are all kinds of religious artifacts, rosaries, crucifixes, Virgin Marys, Last Suppers, Crowns of Thorns, etc. All of them either based in plastic or swimming in faded synthetic three-dimensional lamination like you find a lot in the Deep South. Still, it's not altogether that depressing. In fact the rich smells of Mama's home cooking coming from a tiny kitchen behind the bar make everything seem real promising and warm. We're introduced to Mama right off, and she makes no shortcuts in lambasting you with her generous personality. She's a very wide woman, not very tall but definitely broad and beefy, white hair pulled up and waved and wearing one of those Hawaiian muumuus that stop halfway between her knees and her leathery bare feet. She wears a tiny silver chain around one ankle with a small silver heart resting on a blue vein. She stares up at you from below with an expression halfway between tears and a kind of sentimental good wishing. Later, it turns out that she breaks into sudden fits of tears and sobbing for no apparent reason other than her memory of past love suddenly welling up into the present. Then she immediately cures herself and goes on to show you some tiny object she's collected in her travels, only to break down again in the same emotion-choked delirium. The results are similar to following a slightly demented but benevolent relative around a sanatorium, all the time pretending that everything's okay and masking your true reactions to these manic shifts in her state. There's two recordings of her singing which she brings to our attention, right there on the home juke box. I slide a quarter in and punch the buttons. The first selection is an unending little ditty in a foreign tongue which sounds like a mixture of Spanish and Italian, called ''Mama and God.'' The juke is wired up to an old tin speaker mounted outside on the front porch so that Great Nature can take part in Mama's gifts. There's something fantastic about all this in the way that this woman's life has evolved to this place in the middle of the sticks. Her satisfaction with things as they are and the way she's drawn it all into this tiny world inside the Lounge. A collection of her past which she keeps snugly around her without making her numb to the present.

". . . images of Mama in various stages of her adventurous life."

"The dress fits her like a snake."

As soon as Baez shows up, things really start pumping. Mama immediately relates to Joan's Catholic features and bursts into a series of giggles, sobbing and bear-hugging Joan, then standing arm's length with a firm grip on her shoulders and staring up into her eyes, tears streaming down both cheeks. She squeezes Joan's hand, lifts up her muumuu, and starts sprinting up a narrow flight of carpeted stairs. "Come, I have something to show you. Something I want you to have. Come." Baez is towed into Mama's bedroom, placed on the billowy blue bed just below a large color portrait of Christ while Mama rummages through an old dresser and hauls out a white sequined wedding gown. She wheels the gown around and holds it out to Joan. There is a silent moment of almost religious proportions as Mama slowly tiptoes toward Baez with the dress.

Joan is squirming halfway between embarrassment and glee at the old woman's generosity. "I couldn't take that, Mama. That's yours."

"I want you to have it. It was mine when I was a girl and now I want you to have it."

Joan ducks into a closet and starts changing as Mama forages anew into other drawers for more relics. She pulls out glittering blue necklaces with earrings to match, jeweled brooches, even a green guitar. Joan emerges from the closet in glistening white. The dress fits her like a snake. Mama starts crying at this vision and showers Joan with the jewelry. The cameramen are freaking out from lack of film. Gaffers are running up and down the stairs trying to reload the magazines at atomic speeds. The lights are being changed. Mama

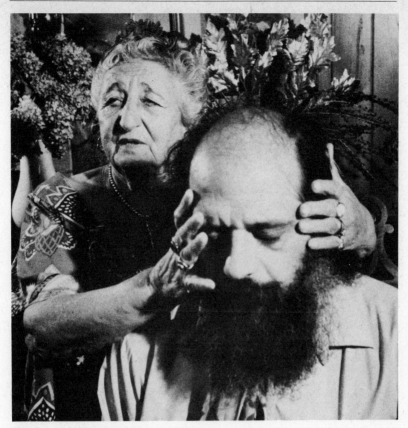

Mama with Allen Ginsberg.

starts rambling on about God and Christ and "luck" and healing and medicine and church and love, and Joan is trying to remain upright through it all. Finally she asks Mama if she'd like to hear a song. Mama nods and Joan goes into a lilting country tune that has Mama mesmerized to the floorboards. She rocks in slow motion on her barefoot heels, eyes rolling back into herself, both hands clasped across her dumpling of a stomach, an expression of pure audio-ecstasy melting down her broad face. Joan's tremolos are ringing off every corner of the old woman's crowded bedroom. For a second everything stands still and just listens.

Downstairs, Dylan and the second bus have arrived. He's already in the midst of an impromptu scene at the bar with Ronee Blakely. Something about him being her groupie. Her a famous singer, and him dogging her shadow clear across the country just to get a glimpse of her in the flesh. Howard's upside down in one corner, dripping sweat, with the camera held between his knees. His crew seems to be in the same frenzied state of unreadiness. The sound man is throwing his equipment across the floor in a desperate effort to reload the tape machine while the lighting guys are strapping spotlights to the hatrack with huge strips of gaffer's tape. Dylan is cruising through his second brandy and seems to be having a good time. He shifts from one leg to the other and bops language over Ronee's head. She does her best to establish a repartee, but there's something stilted about the situation. Then suddenly Baez unfolds in her white visionary elegance and the whole air gets zipped. Here is where the pure chance of things has taken the upper hand and turned out better than anything we could have possibly planned in advance. Joan plants herself at one end of the bar with Dylan at the opposite end. She bears down on him through her black eyes. Dylan twitches slightly, orders another brandy, and grins at the situation sideways. The cameras are rolling for sure. Joan plunges straight into it. "Why did you always lie?"

"I never lied. That was that other guy."

"You're lying now."

The cameras are crackling. Everyone's tiptoeing heavily, doing pantomime slaps on his knees at the outrageousness of this moment. Joan presses on.

"You were always calling me up and lying to me."

"Aw, come off it. You think everything's bullshit. Now I'll admit, there's some things that are definite bullshit but not everything."

"Stop lying, Bobby. You want them to turn the cameras off, don't you?"

"What ever happened to that boyfriend of yours?"

"Don't change the subject."

"I'm making conversation."

Baez beams at him, white teeth flashing over the top of Mama's blue necklace.

"What would've happened if we'd got married, Bob?"

"I married the woman I love."

"And I married the man I thought I loved."

This is turning into either the worst melodrama on earth or the best head-to-head confessional ever put on film. Dylan is dancing around, soaked in brandy, doing his best to dodge the Baez kidney punches. She just stands there, planted, hoisting one-liners at him like cherry bombs. Producers are wincing in the background. Musicians are tittering. Cameras are doing double time.

"Didn't you used to play the guitar?"

"No, that was that other guy."

"What other guy, Bob?"

"That little short guy. I forget his name."

"Oh, you mean that little Jewish brat from Minnesota? His name was Zimmerman."

"Yeah."

"Why'd you change your name, Bob?"

"Just for a change."

"Do you still play the guitar?"

"Yeah. Every once in a while. We've got a road show."

"Oh, yeah, I heard about that. What's it called? Rumbling something?"

"... and bops language over Ronee's head."

"Arlo finally announces that dinner is ready."

"Something like that."

"Where are you playing?"

"Little places. Just around."

Arlo finally announces that dinner is ready. Dylan's not hungry. He wants to go on with the shooting. It's hard to resist the smells of Mama's fish gumbo, so we all pack it in for a while to dive into huge plates of the stuff. Bob is really hot for the film now. He takes his plate into another room and sets up a scene of him eating with Scarlet Rivera, Ginsberg, and Rob Stoner, and Arlo sits down at an old beat upright piano. Dylan starts talking to Scarlet at the table, asking her what goes on in this town. Scarlet picks right up on it and starts winding her way through a "hometown girl" routine. Arlo does a soft piano, silent movie back-up to the dialogue. The camera crews are going bananas trying to keep up with all this shift of scenery, light changes and at the same time balancing plates of gumbo off their elbows, sneaking forkfuls at the same time they're adjusting camera angles. Mama is handing out black-and-white postcards of herself in her younger days. The scene at the table picks up momentum and begins to turn into a full-tilt Max Sennett routine with Jack Elliot appearing in the window singing sea chanties, then Ginsberg reading from *Moby Dick*, then Dylan crawling across the table, out the window and disappearing. Then Stoner appearing with the green guitar doing his Gene Vincent impersonation, then Barry's dog, Miller, appears, crawls through the window, across the table, through plates of fish bones, and leaps to the ground.

Outside, Joan and Dylan are having an intimate scene under a green apple tree, then moving down to a pond and throwing rocks, leaving cameramen broken in their wake. The whole thing has busted loose into this chain reaction of insanity and good times. The film is really happening to the point of almost causing all this collage of inspired events. This stuff wouldn't be going on without a camera around. Not like this anyway.

All of a sudden it's nighttime and someone remembers we have to be somewhere. Another concert somewhere. Mama's Lounge is glowing in the dark, as though the special energies from the day have been transmitted to it, seeping into its walls and boards somehow, causing it to throb with life in the middle of the Massachusetts woods. The bus drivers come out of hibernation behind the wheels. The gear's packed up and we're rolling off again, leaving Mama doing dishes in her muumuu.

Scarlet, the "hometown girl."

"Stoner doing his Gene Vincent impersonation."

If a Mystery Is Solved

If a mystery is solved, the case is dropped. In this case, in the case of Dylan, the mystery is never solved, so the case keeps on. It keeps coming up again. Over and over the years. Who is this character anyway?

Opposite: "Joan and Dylan are having an intimate scene."

"Who is this character anyway?"

Durham, New Hampshire

University of New Hampshire: Neuwirth's street-gang punk band is tighter than ever. Steve Soles's "Don't Blame Me," T-Bone's "Foreign Love," and Stoner's "Wasted." How many bands carry this many jewels of songwriting all coming from separate sources? It's like each guy on his own is a whole band. In fact every one of them has his own band on the side somewhere. Then Ramblin' Jack's beautiful crystal-like yodel comes, transporting you right across the Great Plains. "Good mornin', captain." The "transcendental cowboy." Then Dylan in white face messing with the phrasing of "It Ain't Me," twisting up the rhythm structure, elongating the lines to the point where you think he'll never make it. He'll never fit the thing into the music. Then, at the last minute, it all slides together. Ronson pulling classic country/western licks out of nowhere. Then Dylan grabs his special wicked orange electric Fender and launches into a new version of "Williams and Zinger." Mansfield coloring with beaut mandolin. Dylan shooting from the hips on "Durango." He dedicates it to Sam Peckinpah. Weird spasm with the Fender. He becomes a Haitian devil dancer on "Isis," holding his hat like it's about to take off in a tornado. He creates a third body and sends it up to the ceiling, watching it hang helplessly from the rafters. Stoner comes knifing in on harmony. Everything held firm inside the chopping six-eight time like one of those ancient country-fiddle tunes. Scarlet Rivera, sailing high over the top, sawing at the violin as though she were passing a harpoon through the eye of a needle. McGuinn does "Eight Miles High," classic freak-out of the sixties, with Baez in full-tilt boogaloo from a sitting position on stage beside him. Her black hair shaking to the point of convulsion. She stands and dedicates "Virgil Cain" to "a man who was on a fishing boat this morning and gave me two lobsters." Dylan comes back for second set with a diamond earring dripping down his neck. "Simple Twist of Fate" with his hard cowboy heel driving down into the stage below. As I'm watching this heel of his and seeing the precision of it and hearing the way it resonates clear down through the floor, up through his body, through the song, into the microphone and out into the hall, it suddenly flashes on me that this thing is way beyond pop music. This thing is ancient ritual. The snake dance of the Hopi (before the government sent spies out there with cameras and tape recorders) had, at the heart of it, the idea that the dancers were messengers from this world sending for help to the spirits of another world. A world below the earth, inhabited by snakes. The medium was the dancer's heel as it pounded down in a steady rhythm and sent its human vibrations to the "ones" below. If the heel was heard, then the prayer was answered, usually in the form of a rainstorm. Rolling Thunder is making a sound.

Where Does a Hero Live?

Through bragging, a lot of early-day American heroes sprang up. Paul Bunyan, Pecos Bill, all those mythic guys emerged from fantastic "tall tales," mostly based on macho bravado and superhuman strength. Pecos Bill dug the Rio Grande with his bare hands. Paul Bunyan uprooted mighty trees and drank whole lakes in a single sitting. But these guys were totally fictitious. Then there were the real live ones like Jesse James, Billy the Kid, Mickey Free, Buffalo Bill. Tales grew around them mostly out of a giant communications gap between the stolid intellectual East Coast and the wide-open mysteries of the West. The East was intrigued and curious about all these dudes, and the West was more than willing to supply them with all the fancy embroidered "facts" of their heroism. So, even though they were real guys involved in a real environment, their deeds were largely invented to satisfy this growing hunger and intrigue from the opposite coast. That hunger never left us. Even now, when communications are almost down to teleportation of brain signals, there's still an emotional space in us that needs filling. And it's still the same as it was then. It doesn't matter if the information on our heroes is completely made up, we still want to believe it. Even with the advent of "demystification," we get stoned out on the gyrations of a few individuals. Somebody "out there" is actually doing what cries out in us to be done. Something somehow that we know is in us, but it's not us that's doing it. It's a hero. It's not a hero. It's just a guy or a girl or somebody. But it's them and not us. It's them performing an act that's totally together. We feel the same act in us but it's dormant. It's lying around and undeveloped. So we're all applauding ourselves is what it comes down to. "There it is! Up there! The whole of mankind in one single act!" And he's doing it. He's getting it on for all of us. And he's doing it better than anybody. There's nobody who can touch him in this particular sphere. It's not worship exactly, it's revelation. It's like watching Wilt Chamberlain stuff basketballs in the hoop like he's packing a lunch. It's almost out of the realm of possibility, but he's actually doing it.

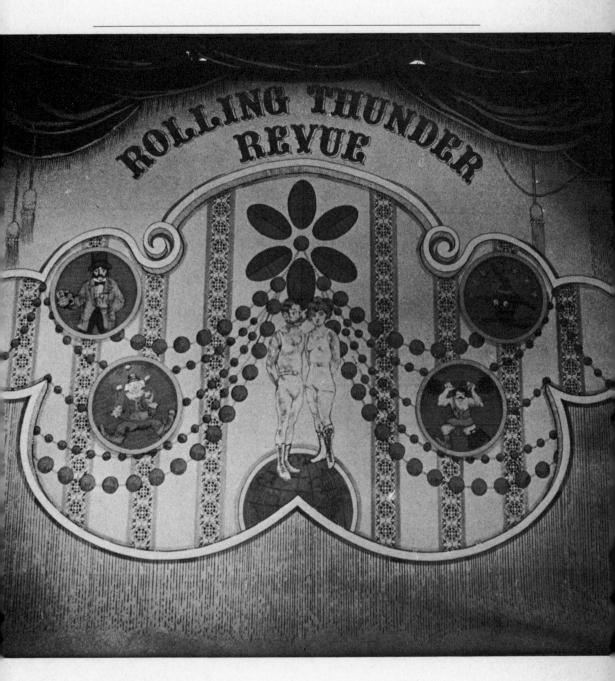

" 'There it is! Up there!' "

Conrad

DYLAN: Have you ever read Conrad?
ME: No.
DYLAN: You should read Conrad.
    (*long pause*)
ME: Do you read a lot?
DYLAN: Some.
ME: Did you always read a lot?
DYLAN: I always read some.
ME: Where'd you get the books?
DYLAN: People's libraries. Just go into people's libraries and they'd have 'em.

Audience

A concert audience has a face. It looks worked upon. Wild eyed. Stimulated from a distant source like a laboratory experiment. As though the stage event, the action being watched and heard, is only a mirror image of some unseen phenomenon. The only protected space is up on stage. Dylan says it's the only time he feels alone. When he's up there. When he's free to work his magic. No one can touch him. No one can sidle up, pretending it's all just an accidental encounter, and pick his brains, his heart, his skin, his flesh and blood. All they can do is imagine what he's like. You see them staring hard into his white mask, his gray-green eyes, trying to pick at the mystery. Who is he anyway? What's the source of his power? An apparition? What kind of person moves like that? Stiff necked from his harmonica brace. Alternate rocking side to side. Keeping equal time on each foot. Now the ragged brown cowboy boots take on the look of huge crow's-feet. A buzzard's legs. He turns into a rooster. A fighting bantam cock. His head outsized for the body. White. Shoulders hunched like a flyweight boxer. Jeans falling down his hips. Dancing backward into black space. Walking completely out of the picture. Hiding behind black Rob Stoner. Disappearing before their very eyes. Re-emerging. Arriving at the mike at the very last fraction of a second. At a moment when any other performer on earth would have already blown it. But now he's minus guitar. Has he lost it? Has he caused it to dematerialize? What's he got in his hand? Then, wham, it's on them before the shock can even register. Harmonica cuts the air like his phantom brother. He adds it like a character to a play. The audience is busted. Their skulls can't take it. The harp sound is awesome in its lonely courage. It cuts into every single soul within earshot. It takes the roof right off and sends this massive human chemistry flying out into the freezing night. Beyond anything they could have expected a week ago when they were scrounging around their bedrooms for seven crummy bucks to buy a seat. Here is the magician. Before their eyes. But now it's not the eyes that see him. It's the heart. It's the heart all along that they were searching for and now he's shown them to it by a sleight of hand. A flash of chrome between his teeth.

"A concert audience has a face": Allen Ginsberg,
Joni Mitchell, and Sara Dylan in front row.

Opposite: "It takes the roof right off."

Hospitality Inn

Stuck away in a corner of this neuterized hellhole is a small room with a sign on the door saying GAMES ROOM. Everyone has migrated to it like a refuge. Joni Mitchell is cross-legged on the floor, barefoot, writing something in a notebook. She bites her lip and looks over to Rick Danko, who's smashing the shit out of a pinball machine with both kneecaps, then pounding on the sides with both fists. Insane games of air hockey, pucks flying across the room and landing on somebody's pool table. The high spirit of competition has seized us all. We keep getting stuck in motels that are miles from anywhere. Totally isolated with no wheels and not even a drugstore within walking distance. The reasons for this seem to be mostly security, but after a while the "cutoffness" of it starts to take its toll. The concert is given in some kind of a city. The audience gets ripped with energy and bursts into the night streets with it. Then we sneak off in unmarked vehicles, secret-agent style, wind our way through narrow back roads, and find ourselves in another prefabricated wonder resort sometimes sixty miles away from the site of the concert. This constant "strike and retreat" style really starts to work on your psyche after a while. The "world out there" takes on a strange unreality, as though it's all being played in a different ball park, in another league. You either feel above it or below it or way off to the side of it, but never a part of it. Headlines in the paper seem like messages delivered from outside the walls. Even headlines that feature the people on the tour. There's nothing that reveals the total myth of newspaper journalism more than being inside the world of the subject being written about. This feeling of separateness weasels its way into everything. Even ordering food in a restaurant takes on a different tone from usual, because you're in the company of something that's so public that even the waiters know about it. You find yourself expanding to the smell of arrogant power or deflating to total depression. You begin wishing you could just go back into the kitchen with the waiter and wash a few dishes or even go back home with him and watch color TV with his grandmother. Anything just to get the taste back of "normal everyday life." The Games Room is going off the deep end. Twenty-dollar bills are being fluttered across the pool tables. Ping-Pong balls crushed into the walls. Bodyguards are pitted against superstars in grim pinball battles. Side bets are being collected. Stud poker is evolving in one corner. Then everything filters away to the elevators. To music. To another marathon night to the break of day.

Opposite: Joni Mitchell.

Pinkeye

D ave Myers, our lead cameraman, has developed conjunctivitis in his camera eye. Although it must be painful for Dave, it only adds to the mounting "buffoon" image that the whole film crew has taken on in the eyes of the musicians. One fuck-up after another keeps compounding on us as though we're doing stand-in bits for Laurel and Hardy. An Indian medicine man called Rolling Thunder showed up all the way from the West and performed a special Tobacco Ceremony at the break of dawn, with all the main stars involved. This was to be a sure-fire sequence in the film and the crew was given special instructions on how to find the location. It was described as a "Disney-type" mansion that "you can't miss," right off the main highway. It turned out that all the mansions have "Disney-type" overtones, and the crew spent all morning trying to track down the one special one but never found it. Another time we dragged everyone out to a replica Pilgrim village in the freezing nighttime only to find out there was no electricity for lighting the scenes, and running the risk of causing pneumonia in the stars. Barry Imhoff is beside himself with rage. "You people are endangering my principles! If this kind of stuff keeps up, I'm just going to cancel the whole film project! That's it! I've had it up to here!"

Opposite: Joni.

David Blue

D avid Blue keeps showing up at different places on the tour. He flies in from his own tour schedule in the South whenever he gets a break. Blue gangster suit, bleary eyed, hoarse throat, wrinkled scarf, he always gives the impression he's trying to repair his health but never quite gets on top of it. He runs a stream of words at us over breakfast. "Yeah, the groupies always get heavier at it than you. They eat you alive. They cop your style then turn it around on you. Hey, you know Dylan's wife Sara is gonna show up in Niagara. You wanna see a heavy chick? Just wait till her and Joni Mitchell get around each other. You'll get some shit on camera then, I can guarantee it. Sara's a very regal, powerful chick, and Joni's gettin' into her empress bag now. I mean Joni's a real queen now. She's really gettin' up there. You just wait until they get in front of the camera."

It turns out they never do. At least not when I was around. At one point there was talk of them doing some kind of Greek Siren scene with the men groveling at their feet, but that never panned out. Somewhere along the line they turned into hookers in front of the camera, along with Joan Baez. I don't know how that happened.

Potential Scenes
for Film

Boxing Match (Imhoff vs. Kemp)
Railroad Boxcar (Dylan and Jack E.)
Sister Reunion (Baez and Blakely)
Jack Elliot—narration on past ten years
Burroughs—magazine cutup (with Dylan in Boston)
E. A. Poe—''Raven'' (Dylan in Boston)
Wyeth—ragtime piano (melodrama in front of Rolling Thunder curtain)
McGuinn—telephoning wife
Golf Course—entire tour playing
''Alabama Song''—entire tour singing
Pool Hall (Dylan)
Thanksgiving Dinner—outdoor feast with entire tour
Poker Game (band members)
Horse Sequence (Ramblin' Jack, etc.)
Superstition Sequence (Scarlet, Baez, Ronee)
Scarlet—fiddle in woods
Acoustic Rehearsal (band)
Miracle Scene
Ginsberg—schoolroom—teaching poetry to the poets
Doc. footage of how band members came in contact with Neuwirth/Dylan
Listening Sequence (Ginsberg, Dylan—listening and naming sounds)
Ginsberg speaking on religion
Ramblin' Jack speaking on various forms of travel—boats, trucks, horses
Speaking-in-Tongues Sequence (Ginsberg, Dylan, Neuwirth)
Allen leading entire cast in meditation
Highway-Hitchhike Sequence
Fishing
Truck Driving (Jack E.)
John Wilkes Booth (Steve Soles—backstage)
Neuwirth/Dylan
Eagle Assassin—Neuwirth
''Hurricane'' Article
Joni Mitchell
Sacco-Vanzetti
Donut Shop (Dylan)
Scarlet in Attic
Napoleon
Burroughs—tracking shot (''Breakers'')
''Thunder lived in the falls''

Fans

Fans are more dangerous than a man with a weapon because they're after something invisible. Some imagined "something." At least with a gun you know what you're facing.

On the Road to Lowell

Allen's in the front, in the nondriver position. Some people who sit in that position, who know how to drive a car, sit differently from those who don't. Allen's one of those who don't. He sits sort of sideways, black, graying curls jumping like little springs over his ears, head bent low over Kerouac's *Mexico City Blues*, stacks of other Kerouac's falling off his knees: *Dr. Sax*, *Visions of Cody*, *Dharma Bums*—all flowing picture words of places we're heading straight into. First glimpse of Lowell off the edge of freeway is the opposite of what you'd call romantic. Smoking black brick skeleton buildings, stacked-up clapboard houses, dirty little parks, brown gymnasiums. We swing off with Allen carrying on a running narration. Kerouac leaping through his childhood. We're being followed this time by a reporter from *Rolling Stone* in a red Galaxy. Driver Jack does a few fancy hangtails and leaves the sleuth behind. We pull up at Nick's Lounge, a depressing little Massachusetts bar owned by Kerouac's brother-in-law, Nick Sampas. Inside there's some kind of police blowout going on for a local candidate for mayor or governor or something. Hard-ass-looking beer drinkers. Everyone juiced in the middle of the day. Crepe-paper decorations, spaghetti à la carte, garlic bread. The place is really loud and in different circumstances would make even a redneck paranoid. Everything's set up for us though, and the Sampas brothers greet us with genuine hospitality and good cheer. Nick Sampas is built like a green quarter horse and talks like you're clear across the room even when you're standing right next to him. Tony is the opposite of his brother. Tall, thin, soft spoken and somehow immediately puts you in mind of William Burroughs. He chain-smokes and talks about his memories of Jack. On the wall, lost in among dozens of snapshots of other locals, is a color Polaroid shot of Kerouac and a girl taken right there in Nick's. Taken about a month before he died. He looks very soused and bloated. We're treated to big plates of spaghetti and cold beer as we run down the different locations we want to hit with Tony. Tony smiles as he hears the names, as though each one brought its own special picture to mind.

We head out in Tony's big station wagon with the heater turned on full blast. Halfway to the cemetery to visit Kerouac's grave, Tony pulls out a tape recorder and a special tape. "This thing was recorded at the bar. I don't think anyone outside the family's ever heard it." He snaps the cassette into place and suddenly there's the voice of Jack. Speaking like a ghost over time. Ginsberg listens with a smile. There it is, right inside a station wagon, captured in his hometown, the rasping whacked-out voice of Kerouac hisself. He's obviously ripped on something because the associations are nonstop, sometimes lilting into an old cowboy song, sometimes beating out the rhythm of language on his knees, trains, drunks, brakemen, California, "the midnight ghost, good codeine, howlin' round the bend, jockeys all ride away in Cadillacs, fields full of potatoes, Santa Clara Valley, Morgan Hill, dippin' into the past, cement factory, looks like Kafka, lettuce bowl of the world, all ya gotta do is git an airplane, fill it with mayonnaise, fly over and drop it, now you shoot up toward the high school." We swing into the graveyard through black iron gates, fresh graves being dug, old names on rock: "Mahoney," "O'Keefe," "Killmarten," "Benoit," "Ti-Jean." We stop.

Lowell Notes

Kingdom of childhood
hometown—innocent
roots—Dr. Sax—origins of the prophet
language
birth and death in same place
rebirth
life after—kingdom after death
dream of world outside
escape to bigger world
return to safety of small world
escape death
protection through religion
superstition
Catholic
religion/fear
escape through travel
Ambrose Bierce
Lafcadio Hearn
speaking in tongues
miracle

Lowell Locations

Grave
Library
High School
Mill Co.
Baptiste Church (what saint will deliver us?)
Moody St. Bridge
Textile Lunch
Orphanage
Grotto
Castle (Dr. Sax)
Birthplace
Nick's Lounge
Pool Hall (play for high stakes—souls and sings sins)

Singing
on the Grave

October –Lowell

Allen quotes from Kerouac's favorite Shakespeare: "How like a winter hath my absence been. . . . What freezings have I felt, what dark days seen!/What old December's bareness everywhere!" It's right close to the time of year he died in. Trees sticking up naked, blankets of blowing leaves. Dylan and Ginsberg perched close to the ground, cross-legged, facing this tiny marble plaque, half buried in the grass: " 'TI-JEAN' [little Jack], JOHN L. KEROUAC, Mar. 12, 1922-Oct. 21, 1969 — HE HONORED LIFE—STELLA HIS WIFE, Nov. 11, 1918—." Dylan's tuning up his Martin while Ginsberg causes his little shoe-box harmonium to breathe out notes across the lawn. Soon a slow blues takes shape with each of them exchanging verses, then Allen moving into an improvised poem to the ground, to the sky, to the day, to Jack, to life, to music, to the worms, to bones, to travel, to the States. I try to look at both of them head-on, with no special ideas of who or what they are but just to try to see them there in front of me. They emerge as simple men with a secret aim in mind. Each of them opposite but still in harmony. Alive and singing to the dead and living. Sitting flat on the earth, above bones, beneath trees and hearing what they hear.

Sam Shepard, Bob, and Allen.

Dylan's Hands

White, wrinkled, double-jointed little finger. Long nails hovering over Allen's harmonium like a tentacle animal. Weathered, milky leather hands that tell more than his face about music and where he's been. Ancient, demonic, almost scary, nonhuman hands.

Stations

Catholic Grotto, Lowell, Massachusetts: Huge cement crucifix bleeding down from a hill overlooking the playground of a French orphanage. Behind it, the river swirling under Moody Bridge. Dylan peering up at Christ face. "What can you do for a guy like that?" Portuguese kids released from class, swarming through glassed-in sculptures of the Stations of the Cross. Southsea-island language hitting the cold air. Old Frenchman soothing his rosary between flat fingers, kneeling in front of the blue Virgin. Ginsberg and Dylan lighting prayer candles in a cave. Cameras tracking them through the playground. Little kids, like insect life, buzzing all around them. Basketballs whizzing past their heads. Kids, shipped in from the voodoo culture, from the fat sunny ocean to the cold white East Coast. Other rich kids shipped from Manhattan. Catholic culture. Dormitories on the sixth floor lined with aisles of neat little white pint-size beds. Crosses all over the green walls. Short basin sinks and toilets. Nuns walking into the camera. Walking into the empty room with a bearded bald man walking in slow motion, arms crossed on his chest, and a dwarf-like caballero sitting on a bed, staring out a blowing window. No talking. Just sitting and walking. Just the whirring of the sixteen millimeter and the shuffle of the Nagra.

Lowell,
Massachusetts

Now, in the face of burned-out Kerouac, Cassady, and all the other ones who went over the hill, this life seems like a miracle. Still ongoing. Ignoring all that. Respecting it but not indulging in remorse. Allen and Dylan singing on his grave. Allen, full of life, hope, and resurrection. Poets of this now life. This here life. This one being lived and living.

Dead and don't know it. Living and do. The living have a dead idea.

Kerouac, *Mexico City Blues*

The Inventor

Dylan has invented himself. He's made himself up from scratch. That is, from the things he had around him and inside him. Dylan is an invention of his own mind. The point isn't to figure him out but to take him in. He gets into you anyway, so why not just take him in? He's not the first one to have invented himself, but he's the first one to have invented Dylan. No one invented him before him. Or after. What happens when someone invents something outside himself like an airplane or a freight train? The thing is seen for what it is. It's seen as something incredible because it's never been seen before, but it's taken in by the people and changes their lives in the process. They don't stand around trying to figure out what it isn't, forever. They use it as a means to adventure.

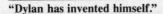

"Dylan has invented himself."

FRIED CLAMS
small 1.50
medium 2.80
large 4.95
FRENCH FRIES
small 50
90

Goat's Island, Newport, Rhode Island

Irate reporter from one of the local rags has brought two cops to arrest Lou Kemp for being "maltreated" by one of the security guards last night. Seems he was prowling his way around the hotel looking for any possible scoops and started clawing on Baez' door at two in the morning. The security jumped him and he's ready to press charges for assault. Lou is an imposing figure by any standards, but he looks especially vicious this morning. Fists stuffed into his black leather pockets, he's nose to nose with the reporter and on the verge of decking him right there in the hotel lobby. Ginsberg leaps to the rescue and kicks Kemp in the ass with a wicked blue high-ankled sneaker. "What're you fighting for?" Ginsberg taunts. Suddenly Kemp's attitude crumples to a smile, and he backs off the trembling reporter. The cops stand around taking notes, totally baffled by who exactly all these people are. Allen's dancing around humming a Buddhist prayer and the buses are being loaded in the background. We roll away, leaving the cops in a heated discussion with the reporter, who still feels he hasn't had his rightful pound of flesh.

Newport.

Pilgrim Fear

They didn't know what they'd find. So they run into this huge continent and beach the boat. But they're scared shitless. Even though they've found what they were looking for, they're still scared. There's crazy naked savages all around them. There's one-eyed pirates lurking in the harbors, licking their lips. There's wild wild animals. All kinds of foreign shadows. Things they hadn't expected. So they pray harder than ever now. They build forts and walls and haul in cannon. They rebuild Europe on a primitive land. Everything's full of possible danger. They don't trust a soul. Even their own kind are burned as witches. They lynch Indians at the drop of a hat. They fire wildly into the night. They jump at shadows. They don't play after dark. They bury their dead in secret, in the dead of night, so as not to let the "enemy" know they're weakening. They start dying off. New ships roll in to replace the dead. They're determined to continue. Nothing's going to stop them now. Come hell or high water they're going to persist. They're going to spread themselves no matter what. But now they've forgotten why they came in the first place. Talking to God is out of the picture, because now they've got to exist. Now they've just got to stay alive.

Costume List

3 cowboy vests
2 cowboy coats
2 chaps
1 cowgirl
1 dance-hall girl
1 Indian girl
1 Indian suit
1 sorcerer
1 Napoleon
1 Josephine
1 Rhett Butler
1 Scarlett O'Hara
2 Confederate jackets
2 Union jackets
1 angel top   wings   halo
1 opera cape
3 pioneer dresses
1 French maid
1 Socrates
1 Nefertite

Providence, Rhode Island

The home of the Vanderbilts. Strange sensation of visiting the ghosts of the privileged class and us, a class of privileged nomads, sometimes verging on spoiled-brat status. Plenty of opportunities for radical juxtaposition with scenes of Jack Elliot in cowboy gear waving from a hundred-foot-high balcony to the peons below. Emerald lawns falling away gently across acres to the blue Atlantic. Sculptured hedges. Joan Baez appearing from behind them straddling the shoulders of a mammoth black security guard named Gene, who, in spite of the obvious racist leaps of imagination, resembles a handsome Joe Frazier with a more intelligent eye. T-Bone is lining up a tee shot off the front lawn of a hacker's dream. He misses four times straight with the cameras rolling, slashing black scars of dirt into the gardener's pride. As soon as the cameras switch off he hits a beautiful arcing three hundred yarder which would cause even Nicklaus to cream in his Jantzen sportswear, then he throws himself spread-eagled, face down into the lawn, and bites the dirt. Neuwirth has hit upon an avant-garde shot of himself crawling slowly toward the camera lens on his belly, in search of a rock. Ernie Eagle has broken all the rules by leaving the camera on at hip level while cruising deep within the interior of the ancient haven. (No cameras allowed.) We plant Howie Wyeth on the steps of the cottage built especially for the Vanderbilt kiddies, right between two marble gargoyles. He peers out underneath his slouched cap, reading from the drug experiences of Sir Arthur Conan Doyle.

This right here is history. This right here is beyond any fiction. To place ourselves for even a second inside the drifting leisure time of the super-wealthy of the early days who slipped up here in unimaginable slinky yachts from New York Harbor and docked their noses silently into this plush grass. And now there's this new version of chic running all through a museum, secretly filming right into the depths of their privacy, which is now long gone. It boggles the brain cells to conjure up another scene fifty years from now. Maybe there'll only be black plaques in the ground marking where the buildings once stood.

Providence.

Hotel Crypt

I t's not long before the nucleus of us takes its shape. Who's who in the galaxy of things. A small band with all the implications of the Big One. The world we slide through like it's never there. But now it seems reversed. Like we're not there and all around us life is going on about its business. Waitress serves and goes back home. Back to REAL LIFE. Back to MOM and DAD or KIDS or HUSBAND or both or all. And us sitting. Us sit eating crab legs in a hotel crypt.

Hand Jive
on the Pedal Steel

The band's working through a lazy, back-country tune. You couldn't call it rehearsal, because they're all having too much fun at it. Dylan sits in an old armchair chewing on a liverwurst sandwich and watching them from a distance. He nods his head to the chord changes. Some others are sitting around chewing on food and playing the Pong machine for high stakes. Gary is collecting a bundle and growing in his expertise and finger technique, using two hands and spinning ricochet mind-benders off the forecourt, defying even the laws of computers. Suddenly Dylan leaps to his feet, throws down the liverwurst, and sprints straight toward the vacated slide guitar. He straddles the seat, running his tongue over his teeth, picks up the heavy chrome bar, and starts trying to find the right notes and scales to fit the tune. A few heads turn but no one seems to be expecting much. Hawaiian guitar isn't exactly his forte. The band keeps on as Dylan keeps fishing for the notes, just missing them over the top and bottom. He keeps the volume down so as not to destroy the entire progression that the band has going. He bends lower and lower over steel strings as though trying to see right down inside the thing, between the gaps somewhere, like a mechanic about to lift the entire block out of a small foreign car. He keeps at it diligently for about ten minutes; each moment seems to verge on the possibility of him suddenly finding the whole thing in a flash of inspired genius. Instead, what happens is that he makes a loud exhale, rears backward, turns up the volume, and unleashes a series of random John Cage noises. The band never shows a ripple and moves right into it. Dylan's hand is stroking up and down the length of the strings, the other hand picking at it as though it were a distant bowl of cold chop suey. The Pong game keeps on to the deafening roar of New England jazz-jambalaya-rock'n'roll'n.

Following page: ". . . through a lazy back-country tune."

Danbury, Connecticut

Ethan Allen Hotel

I'm extra horny for a car. Walking is suspicious in a place like Danbury. There's not even dirt banks on the sides of the road. I try hitching three miles into town but wind up hoofing the whole route. Stop in for a chocolate egg cream at the local pharmacy-diner. News in color on TV. Gun shop across the street. I strike up words with a guy about the rising popularity of dog tracks in New England. "There's a new one coming to Connecticut. The horsemen don't like it though. Bad for business." The cook shifts the channel to a William Bendix movie. "No roughhouse in here or you'll get a face full a knuckles," says William. Everyone's hiding behind the *Daily News*. The pock-faced waitress is smoking, bored. Cook moves to the Belmont Racing Form. This could be the 30s or 40s easy. But it isn't.

Dylan on the *Mayflower*.

Inside
a Replica City

Inside a replica city of "the way it was then." At night. With open fires blazing. Dirt floors. Freezing. Mick Ronson in rock and roll shirt sleeves. Blue lips. Bobby Neuwirth has discovered an old gun-slinging brother of a friend of his from way back. He hauls him over through the flickering shadows. The guy is huge and silent. Dressed like a Pilgrim with a beard. Neuwirth swears he's the fastest quick-draw artist in the entire world. So fast in fact that they were trying to hustle him down to Vegas just to put on a show against all takers for the sake of a little gamble. We line him up for the next day on the beach with the cameras to catch all the action. Also, on top of his gun-wheeling talents, it turns out he's an H. P. Lovecraft scholar and knows every New England nook and cranny of the old guy's creepy haunts.

Next day: We meet him on the beach. Jack Elliot has found himself marooned at the very top of the mast of the replica *Mayflower*, and we have no recourse but to leave him to it. He's barefoot and waving silently to the entire assembly below. We move down to a rocky beach where our gunfighter is preparing himself for the first take. Cameras home in on him from a distance of maybe fifty yards. He's got his bearings now and begins his march. Cameras rolling. He comes to the crucial spot, snaps the forty-five out of the holster, but suddenly to the dismay of all onlookers (especially Neuwirth) he DROPS THE GODDAMN PISTOL RIGHT IN THE SAND.

Dylan has wandered off up the street, following a strange waif of a woman dressed in an embroidered blanket with an accordion strapped to her back and singing ancient unheard-of sea chanties in a half-whispered voice.

42nd Street
Face Lift

Tonight Dylan appears in a rubber Dylan mask that he'd picked up on 42nd Street. The crowd is stupefied. A kind of panic-stricken hush falls over the place. "Has he had another accident? Plastic surgery?" Or is this some kind of mammoth hoax? An imposter! The voice sounds the same. If it is a replacement, he's doing a good job. He goes through three or four songs with the thing on, then reaches for the harmonica. He tries to play it through the mask but it won't work, so he rips it off and throws it back into the floodlights. There he is in the flesh and blood! The real thing! A face-lift supreme! It's a frightening act even if it's not calculated for those reasons. The audience is totally bewildered and still wondering if this is actually him or not.

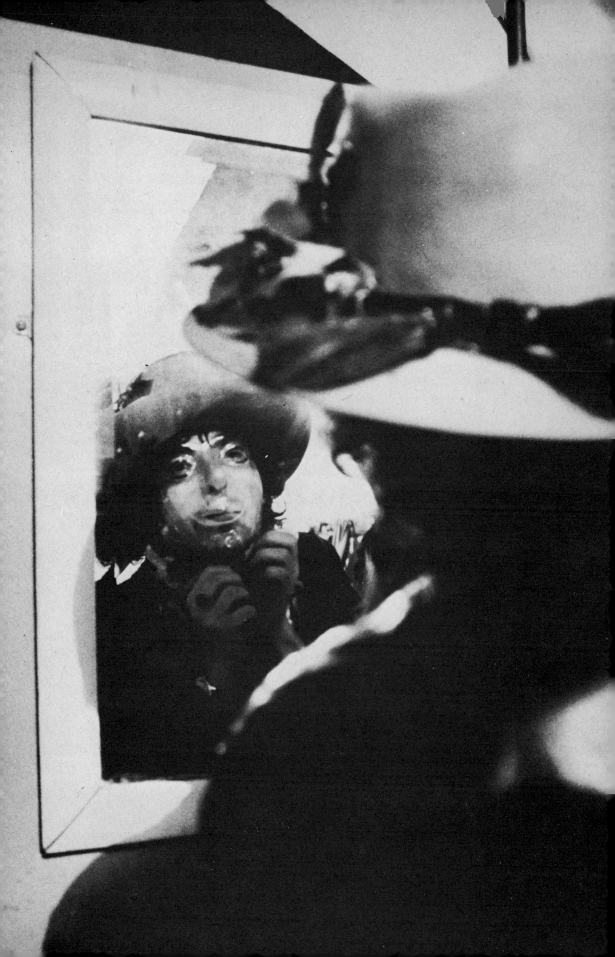

Explore

All the land has been discovered. Some parts of hidden South America maybe still lie out of sight, but this land here has been discovered. Every inch. Now the move is inner space. New religions. est. Gurus. Meditation. Outer space is too expensive and only lies within the reach of the government or corporate industry. Where does Rolling Thunder fall in all this? It's too simple to write it off as just another good-time tour revolving around the mysterious presence of Dylan. There's too many elements involved that keep it swinging off in unforeseen directions. Even if its first intentions weren't to start an expedition, it's turning into that because of something coming from all these people. Everybody's been through something to arrive at this point. Ginsberg's not just along for the ride after going through America backward and forward for over forty years. After seeing close friends die away from him. After sitting with burning corpses on the shores of the Ganges. Baez has spent nights in a bomb shelter in Hanoi during the worst air raid of the war, marched on the Pentagon, still holds beliefs in the power of pacifism, watched her "public image" like it belonged to another person. And Dylan hasn't exactly been in a coma all these years. So what's the story? Beyond the impact of everybody's individual charisma and personality, something is lurking. It's as though we all can smell it but nobody can put a finger on it. It's almost got to be that way so that the search can continue. Gregory Corso once described poetry to me as "a magic probe." He said, "A poet takes it all on. The whole shot." If poetry has the power of transforming emotions the same way music does, then at the same time it has to be discovered halfway in the dark. It discovers itself. It lets itself be known through the revelation of the poet. At the same time Dylan is helping people, he's being helped. This camaraderie is growing.

Famous Curtain Trick

Shifty Jacques Levy, who blitzed off-off-Broadway some years back with his head-on Brechtian style, is responsible for at least one theatrical bravado act. It's a trick that totally works. A sight-and-sound gag that every single audience on the tour wets their pants over. Here's how it works. Dylan finishes the first set and leaves the stage smoking. Neuwirth steps up to the mike and tells the screaming mob that Dylan will be back in fifteen minutes. Curtain drops and it's intermission. An act break. Just like uptown except in this case the audience retires to blow a few j's instead of munching on five-dollar Cadbury chocolate bars. Fifteen minutes are up. Audience are back stomping on their metal folding chairs. Suddenly the houselights dim. Audience begin to roar, but then something happens. From out of the roar two acoustic guitars are heard. Where are they coming from? Then two voices come into it. A male and a female. But where's it coming from? The audience begin to listen and quiet down, but they can't see the source of this sound. They strain toward the stage but the curtain's still down. Now the voices take on characters. It's definitely Dylan, but who's the chick? Then they understand in a flash. They understand with the ears alone. That high, totally female sound is backing him up. Not just backing him up but becoming one voice with him. Visions of Martin Luther King, Washington, D.C., 1964, Kennedy, Birmingham, a flood of images belonging to a whole decade come riding on the words of "Blowing in the Wind." The curtain slowly rises and there they are revealed. Baez and Dylan, like the right and left hand of an American epic. The audience goes right off the deep end. The song they're singing can't even be heard through this thunder of emotion. The singers are doing a pantomime in front of an ocean of applause. Baez looks perfect. Like a trim athlete in a black velvet coat, jet black Mexican hair cut much shorter than in her folksy days. She seems completely with Dylan in a way that no one else who sings with him can ever be. It's as though she knows his every move just from having been there before. She doesn't have to stare at his mouth in order not to be caught off guard by his changes in phrasing. She knows it in the bones somewhere.

"Jacques Levy, who blitzed off-off-Broadway some years back."

Raw Meat

Strange fear comes over me that the audience might actually devour Dylan and the band. It seems that close. I'm afraid for them. Just the thought that I might be a witness to it. The whole audience takes on the shape of an animal. No more singles, just a throbbing mass, fierce and being teased by raw meat. They make a sound together like a primitive rumble. They crush Styrofoam cups, they chew on blankets, bottles smashing in every corner. I'm getting out fast. Into the night.

Niagara Falls

A hundred bucks' worth of Valiums are delivered to the Niagara Hilton like so much Chicken Delight. They come complete with a little pharmacy man in a blue baseball cap, overcoat, and galoshes. Each prescription in its own little white pharmacy envelope with the customer's name in longhand. The doctor was here this morning, sitting in his own special room with his own special needle, pumping everyone full of vitamin B. I took a hit myself. Did nothing for me. Not to say that it's all a Vitamin Hoax.

This is possibly the worst hotel yet. One of those monsters they haven't finished yet, but one day it's intended to be something really fantastic. It's intended to be so fantastic, in fact, that no matter what, when you take a key at this joint, you're guaranteed not to know where you are until the day you leave.

November 13, New Haven, Connecticut

Pasolini's Murder in the Paper

He reached for the kid's crotch. Seventeen-year-old kid. Kid freaks. Outrage. Beats him unconscious. No idea who he's beating. Just some horny old guy. Drives over his head with a sports car. New Haven is a fake town. Two concerts sold out. Filled to the brim. Violence breathes through the skin. College types going to see the prophet. Because of the closeness to New York, the New Haven concert attracts some of the bigwigs like Albert Grossman, Bill Graham, and Patti Smith, who shows up looking like a samurai warrior on welfare. Joni Mitchell flies in from the Coast and tunes up in the bathroom. Dylan is a magnet. He pulls not only crowds but superstars. Who wouldn't play with Dylan if he asked them? Even Yehudi Menuhin would if Dylan didn't already have a gypsy on the fiddle. Neuwirth is pacing around the dressing room like a poisoned cat. Chomping at the bit. Make-up dripping down his eyes. Growling at the beefed-up atmosphere backstage. I can definitely sympathize with his attitude. It seems to me that musicians, no matter what, should get some breathing space just to themselves before they go on to crank out two to four hours' worth of music for a raving, lunatic audience of strangers. It's lopsided to think that if a person gets thousands of people emotionally off the deep end the way these audiences get, that person isn't also paying a big price in terms of his own energy. Meanwhile the backstage areas are filling up fast.

Joni Mitchell

Here's someone who just appears, just walks out with a plain guitar, a beret, and a history of word collage. Every single time the place goes up in smoke like a brush fire. She stands there in the midst of it, making believe she's tuning an already well adjusted guitar until the place calms down. No doubt the element of surprise, of the audience not knowing she's on the bill, is partly responsible for the explosions, but there's something more important in it—the fact that people listen to her every word. Her music's nothing outrageous, but her word maneuverings tend to verge on uncanny. "I got a head full of quandry and a mighty, mighty, mighty thirst." She seems to have merged into a unique jazz structure with lyrics and rhythmic construction and even managed to bite the masses in the ear with it.

Opposite, top: Joni with Allen.

Opposite, bottom: Joni, Bob, and McGuinn.

450 Bus Miles

After double New Haven concerts we're in the bus at 1:00 in the a.m., ready to roll 450 miles to Niagara. Gene, the bodyguard, is pacing the aisles, saying that if he doesn't get a bed to himself he's gonna take one with somebody in it. "I don't mind. I used to sleep with four sisters and two brothers. I don't mind a bit." One of the accountant girls rolls over and Gene hauls his hulking frame into the cot. Actually, these buses are a great improvement on the Greyhound style. At least half of us get the chance to be horizontal long enough to cop a few z's. There's a few turkey sandwiches and orange juice passed around. We head out into the freezing night with Ginsberg improvising on the harmonium, chanting a mournful Blake poem to the hum of the diesel. Ronson is wrapped in a coonskin coat and trying to unwind. We hit heavy snow about 4:00 a.m. and the bus eases to a slow canter. The drivers stop for coffee. I remember this gypsy life now. It all floods back from days when I was acting in a traveling road show. Doing one-nighters on Protestant church altars. Sleeping in strange families' empty bedrooms. Packing up and heading out again. Just the mobility of it brings the pulse of high adventure. Even if all we're doing is going up and down the face of New England like Lewis and Clark, lost explorers searching for the wide extremes where land meets water and disappears again. We haul into a Ho-Jo's for a daybreak breakfast of saran-wrapped donuts and tea-colored coffee. The local zombies are all agog at the vision of Ronson looking like a stand-in for Marlene Dietrich, blue eye make-up, teased blond hair stiff with spray, and raccoon coat held tight under the chin. Baez is in top condition and looks like she's just come from a week's rest in Florida, her great laugh rocking through this plastic outpost. Just the thought that we're not stuck in this joint forever is a great liberation.

Bus Notes

Owe Mel 20
room: 817—Dave Myers
909—Larry Johnson

"I'm so horny not even the crack of dawn is safe."

Pawcatuck
Falmouth
Taunton—R.R. 4 (dog track)

manuscripts Kerouac (in brother's possession or bank)
St. Jean Baptiste

"demonic incantations"
"spectral evidence"
sitting on chest
"monster birth" (fornication with Devil)
"witch's familiar"
messenger in cahoots
catbird

Bridget Bishop of Salem (convicted witch—hung 1692)
Mayflower—Jack/Bob
Plymouth Rock—Jack/Allen
shoot village bonfire

alchemist
disguises
Poe
Melville
Ronee sitting on Blue's chest
"Just Like a Woman"
some of preacher (shades, white hair)
preacher slug-out
"Some things are not solvable"
"It's a radio problem"

Stockbridge, Massachusetts

Ronee Blakely is telling me how she's almost died four times in her life. Once by fire, once by choking, and two others I can't remember. It's my birthday and I'm sitting in front of three cakes, a giant pen, a stuffed sex-frog, and other assorted goodies. This is supposed to be the hometown of Norman Rockwell, and the film crew is trying to set up a scene of Rockwell painting Dylan's portrait. It's very artsy-craftsy around here. The hotel is the Red Lion Inn, one of those ancient roadhouses with brass beds and ropes hanging out the windows for fire escapes. The floors are warped to the degree of making you feel you're on board the *Titanic* and everything's in candlelight. Out front, the police have captured two local teen-age hoods who have absconded with some antique wicker chairs from off the hotel's front porch. The cops are methodically taking the chairs out of the guy's trunk and replacing them one at a time. The manager is standing by smugly.

Later, I'm in the darkened dining room alone with Lou Kemp, having a secret meeting about "what's needed to get this film off the ground." His idea is to bring in Coppola or Orson Welles and have him take over the whole shot. "We're after heavyweights, you understand." I understand but I don't agree.

Burlington, Vermont

"**R**ight now a storm cloud has bursted on a Vermont Parking Lot. Busses are standing in it. Arrangements are being made with an eccentric gun collector to transport secretly in the rain a certain personage who may or may not be doing mysterious movements of the tongue accompanied by ancient rhythmic trance dances for the devouring of the MASSES. The feeling is that the weather has busted things wide open and yet due to the extreme level of fantasy contained within our ranks the atmosphere is no concern of ours. We are being moved to Maine. We are an animal."

Slim Shadow, *Zebra Phantom Newsletter*

Dream of a Kid in Vermont Who Couldn't Get a Ticket

"I was watching him sitting on a couch. One of those stuffed kinda brown couches that a dog's eaten part of. You know, the stuffing coming out and everything. Right beside him is a brass spittoon. He's sitting sideways on the couch with some kinda overcoat across his legs. A raincoat. I look up at him and he's got black hair. Greasy. He's got something on his chest that's green. I don't know what it is at first and then I see that he's got tits. Green tits and they have patterns on them like they were molded from one of those Jell-O presses. In fact, the tits look like green Jell-O, sort of shaking all by themselves. He's asking me to go downstairs and pick something up for him. Some kinda food or something. I think it's bagels. Yeah, it's bagels that he wants. And some pemmican. What do you call it—beef jerky. I start to leave but he's calling to me. He seems very sexy, like he's seducing me or something. I start going over to him but I'm sort of scared. I think he's trying to seduce me."

E. A. Poe

Contacts are made with a strange Lower East Side pool hustler who supposedly does amazing impersonations of Edgar Allen Poe. Since the tour is due to strike Boston, we thought it would be a perfect opportunity to find Poe's original house there and put Dylan in a scene with him. We invite the guy to the hotel for a sampling of his talents. He enters the room, a short, balding, nondescript fellow with a small suitcase containing his Poe costume. He retires to the bathroom for the transformation. We're also thinking about the possibility of getting Burroughs into this scene somehow, him maybe doing a cutup collage with Dylan and Poe. Burroughs wants his money in front though and also to have a formal dinner with Dylan in order to get to know him before we do any filming. Dylan is backing off from the whole idea. Suddenly Edgar Allan Poe emerges from the bathroom, an absolute dead-ringer. It's amazing. Shifty eyes, black tails, ruffled cuffs, the entire essence of Poe down cold. Even though we've asked the guy to do something less well known than ''The Raven,'' as soon as he steps out of the bathroom he's into the first stanza: "Once upon a midnight dreary, while I pondered weak and weary . . ." There's no way of stopping him now. Besides, he's totally hypnotic in his delivery. He's got all the demonic obsession of Poe coursing through him. Everyone's pinned to the corners of the hotel room while Poe rants on through his paranoid vision. It's an electrifying private performance that, once again, we fail to get on film. By the time we hit Boston things were so frantic in the film department that we never did get Poe into the action. The little guy packs up his bag and leaves.

Burroughs

GINSBERG: So what about Bill Burroughs? I think he would be great in the film.
DYLAN: But what can he do?
GINSBERG: He'll just be himself.

Into the Combat Zone

I'm walking the Boston pavement in the rain on a strange drug called Lomotil—an opium derivative designed to counteract the "trots." There's many unforeseen side benefits to these little white pills, such as elongated color perception, high pain tolerance, a certain sense of predetermination in all muscular activity, and a wonderful warm glow in the frontal lobe. Right beside me is a mad-dog reporter from *Rolling Stone* named Sloman who's coerced me into leaving the Dylan concert and going out to try to find the Tubes concert in the pouring rain. I call it "concert hopping," or "slumming" in this case, since we're heading into definitely rougher territory than what we left behind. "The combat zone" is the way Sloman names it. Sloman is the supreme master of tack and bad taste. I've never seen one to match him. Not even Harry Katoukas, who was prone to attempting suicide on stage with a dead parrot strapped to his head. Sloman is in a class of his own. He's a New Yorker, but somehow he's made contact with every owner of every strip joint, porn shop, bad-news corner in this town. He's yanking me into doorways and introducing me to the owners like I'm his long-lost kid brother. Silicone-tit blondes are dancing on the bar behind him. "Whad'ya think, Sam? Nice, huh? Nice pair a knockers, huh? Come on, let's get outa here. I wanna show ya some more. Come on." We crash out into the rain again. "What I really wanna find is this great sixty-three-year-old schizophrenic dyke name Ethel. I think her name was Ethel. She disappeared on me. Great chick! Fantastic chick! I wanted to introduce her to Dylan. Let's go in here." We dive into a super brightly lit up sex shop. Everthing's bouncing off the walls. "Let's buy Dylan a present. Come on." He heads for the back of the shop with the salesman. "Have you got anything for a birthday present for a very special guy?" The salesman heads for a stack of yellow boxes in the back. "Well, how special is he? Twelve inches? Ten inches? You gotta give me some hints." Sloman lets out a hyenalike shriek as the salesman starts setting various demonstration models up on the counter. Boxes of dildos, plastic motorized cocks, religious figures with rising members. Sloman's cackling and lifting each one of them toward me for inspection. "How 'bout this one? You think he'd like this one? Whad'ya think?" I can't think. The entire place is doing cartwheels off my brain cells. My body is walking toward the door, my head's on the ceiling somewhere. Sloman's buying a toy monk whose joint springs out between his habit when you squeeze him. The thing I can't figure is, who would ever squeeze a monk?

I'm heading up the street in slow motion asking potential muggers where the Tubes concert is. Most of them don't talk and just point in a daze farther up the bleak pavement. I keep walking. This seems like it's taking a lot longer than it should. Sloman catches up. His silk Philippine jacket is soaked through, so that the lining looks like the outside and the outside looks like it's melted down his pants legs. His green tie is turning into a dripping rope and his white-and-brown brogans are reminding me of Emmett Kelly. In fact his whole person looks like a soggy pretzel disguised as a human. Through some miracle we arrive at the hall where the Tubes are playing, and I suddenly realize that I couldn't care less about even seeing the Tubes. I couldn't care less if I never ever see them, in fact. The only reason for even starting this sojourn is because one of the girls in it is a friend from San Francisco and I just felt like seeing a friend. But this is turning into a nightmare. Right in front of the hall two big beefy guys are slugging it out with each other while some other beefy guys stand around watching. There's blood running with the rain right across the steps of the place. We slide in past the guards, who are also playing audience to the fisticuffs. We start flashing our Rolling Thunder plastic laminated passes around like they were press cards to the White House or something. We're admitted to the monster show. "White Punks on Dope." It's like walking into a crypt festival. TV sets flashing all over the place, violent distorted feedback that sounds like a cow stepping on her afterbirth and not knowing what hit her. An eight-foot transvestite in stilted platform heels, silver skin-tight jumpsuit, teased blond hair, and the drummer behind slashing away at his kit as though he was caught in his own mosquito netting. If this is supposed to be satire, I don't get it. If it's not, then somebody's in bad shape.

We weasel our way backstage with the passes and inquire about Jane from San Francisco. "Who? Never heard of her. You guys aren't supposed to be back here!" "She also goes by the name of Lila the Snake." The guy's not buying it. "Get outa here before I bust yer head open!" Behind him I see Jane coming off stage completely naked except for a couple of buttons and some panty hose. I yell out to her and she escorts us up a metal spiral staircase to the dressing room, followed by four other equally naked girls. Sloman wastes no time in breaking out his instant-erecting toy monk and an assortment of other ingenious sex objects. The girls are unimpressed. Long lines of snow are being inhaled across a record jacket. The place is hot enough to raise mushrooms in and I feel like I'm melting. I leave Sloman and make my way through the horror show back toward the music hall where the Dylan concert is. Strange thoughts are going through me. "What are all these kids doing watching this shit when they could be hearing good music? What do they care about good music? What do they care about a bunch of West Village folk singers from the sixties? They wanna see some action. They wanna see brains dripping from

The Combat Zone.

the ceiling. Is this that generation stuff that you hear about all the time? What's going on anyway? Am I a part of the old folks now? Is Dylan? Is Dylan unheard of in certain circles? Like Frank Sinatra? Bing Crosby? Is this time flying? Is this time flying right past us on all sides? Can anybody see what's really going on?" Not me.

Gypsy

In front of every fancy hotel we stay in, Dylan's big green-and-white camper is parked conspicuously, transforming whatever place it is into a funky kind of trailer-camp atmosphere. He seems determined to maintain his gypsy status at all cost. On Madison Avenue, in the heart of jewelry stores, the camper hums with a secret life. Right across the street the entire Rolling Thunder entourage is holed up in plush suites. The "Chief" sits in his trailer peering out at business life. Sometimes faint acoustic sounds are heard, the chime of bells, strange blue smoke sneaks into the atmosphere. On the side of the camper is a small black-and-white plastic sign that reads KEMP FISHERIES. In one window is a poster for a wrestling match. It could be anybody's guess who's inside the thing.

Connecticut Blues

Feel myself nose diving into negativity. Just wanna go back home. Be in the mountains. Near horses. Near my woman. Back. The organization of the film has fallen into smithereens till it has no shape or sense. No way of planning a day's shooting. Everything's at the mercy of random energy. Ideas flying every which way but no plan. Meetings up the ass. Meetings in oval-shaped, U.N.-style conference rooms, so the sense of self-importance permeates you beyond control. More talk of shooting concerts. More talk on how to organize scenes. How to get Dylan into the picture. Sara. Joni Mitchell. Baez. It's almost that the sheer overkill of available talent is busting us wide open. No one knows where to begin. No information is fed through a common source. Everyone wanders off to rooms, to dining rooms, to front desk, to rent-a-cars, to buses, to game rooms, to bars, to pools, to hospitality suites, to nowhere. Meeting ends. Snow is flying in Connecticut. Buses move out to Hartford concert. Rick Danko and Sandy Bull have joined up now. Like metal shavings on a magnet. My disinterest kills me. Why aren't I blasting off with them to hear all that great music? I've heard it already. But it's not that. It's not having an ax. Being a backstage parasite. Running headless through the dressing rooms. Watching everyone get loaded. Dancing through packs of concert freaks with my plastic I.D. card bouncing from a silver neck chain. Getting the nod from security dudes. Grabbing handfuls of dried fruit, nuts, making notes as a means to stay sane. But I'm not. I'm cracking up behind this. My body quakes from it. This is truly being transported back to the mid-sixties when crystal meth was a three-square diet with "yellow jackets" and "black beauties" for chasers. Not just the sixties of the imagination but the actual body-and-mind sixties. The shattered feeling. I DON'T WANT TO GET BACK TO THE SIXTIES! THE SIXTIES SUCKED DOGS! THE SIXTIES NEVER HAPPENED! Color TV is my only hope now. Room service. The sanctity of pastel hotel suite with two double beds and no people. Chained door. California's long gone. California's over the hill. Los Angeles is burning far off in the papers. Pacific. Blue. Ocean. Far off.

"I don't want to get back to the sixties."

Bob and Stoner.

Acton, Massachusetts

Neuwirth is losing his voice. He's sounding more and more like a bullfrog on a bender. Stoner's got the runs. Myers is nauseated and I'm not feeling too good myself. We all pile into a rented Plymouth Fury and head for the Acton Medical Center. Raven is driving and trying to make the best out of playing nursemaid. We brodey into the parking lot with Neuwirth hacking up yellow lungers and Stoner bitching about he'd better not have to wait and "Why didn't they have the doctor come to the hotel?" Once inside, the waiting room is not to be believed in contrast to our rampaging intestinal condition. Lots of mothers sitting on tweed couches reading *Redbook* while their sniveling offspring do push-ups off the side of the aquarium. Everything's totally quiet and in waiting except for the tittering kiddies. Neuwirth is seized suddenly by an attack of the lower stomach and lurches off toward the bathroom shouting, "I GOTTA CRAP! WHERE'S THE DAMN SHITTER! I GOTTA GO NUMBER TWO REAL BAD!" This goes over real big with the locals as they watch him go staggering by, heading toward the rear of the building. Stoner in his solid-black rocker outfit is trying to straighten out the appointment book with the nurse behind the desk. "There's no reason we should wait. We got a gig to do in two hours. Go tell the doc that we need some shots. I ain't gonna feel real till I feel that steel." The nurse is struggling to retrieve the appointment book and totally aghast at the brash intrusion. Raven's cooling things out, leading Stoner to a soft chair and selecting a current magazine for him. "Here's one on how to build your own flagstone patio." Myers stands numbly by rubbing his blue knitted sailor's cap and blinking at all the funny people. Finally the doc shows up and everyone goes charging in at once except for Neuwirth, who's snuck out the back somehow and disappeared off down the road. Raven shoots out the front door after him. "Neuwirth, goddamnit! The doctor's ready now! Get your ass back here!" Neuwirth yells over his shoulder from the highway. "Tell him I've already died! It's too late!"

Danbury, Connecticut

Ethan Allen Motel

After the concert everyone returns to find his luggage, beds, and other personal items vanished and in their place are someone else's luggage, beds, and personal items. It's one of those college-dorm-type fraternity-club jokes played for the benefit of the filming, but in this case the film crew misses it completely. They're all off somewhere shooting a dog track. In the "hospitality room" is a lone hamster in a green cage. He's a black-and-white furry little beast with a label around his neck, "The Zebra Phantom." The hooch starts flowing freely in the hospitality room and everyone seems to be getting thoroughly plastered on Jack Daniel's and assorted creamed Kahlúa. Ginsberg comes bursting into the party waving *Iron Man* comic books above his head. "Who put comic books on my altar!" No one seems to claim credit for the injustice. Neuwirth breaks in unleashing a fire extinguisher across everyone's lap, and Stoner leaps to the rescue, seizing the fire extinguisher by the throat. A wild struggle ensues, resulting in a cut thumb on Stoner's picking hand. This starts him on a long lamentation on how this new injury is going to affect the quality of the music for the rest of the tour. He goes in search of Band-Aids and iodine. Scarlet is practicing her fiddle scales up and down the hallways, in a long black dress, black snakes painted on her cheekbones. The rest of the party dissolves into private rooms to watch the basketball game on color TV.

Chaos in
the Gun Museum

I'm in a big cement culvert at the bottom of a creek bed looking out across the highway to a gun museum, blinking in the dark. The place is owned by a weird chiropractor who collects all kinds of ancient weapons and instruments of torture. Black rubber dolls with gun barrels hidden in their stomachs so that when you squeeze them they shoot you. Mandalas of rifle cartridges imbedded in plastic resin tabletops, which "guests" eat their fancy dinners off of. Full-scale mummies and skeletons hanging from the rafters, surrounded by swords and machetes. They're trying to film a scene in there with Dylan and Neuwirth. Some kind of *Maltese Falcon* take-off. Customers started showing up for dinner and the feeling was like being in the midst of a bad Vincent Price ritual. I took off down the road hoping to find one of those typical American diners for a fast cup of java, but the gun-museum restaurant seems to be the only commerce on the highway. I heard running water and hung a fast left off the pavement and found myself down here at the bottom. Very quiet. Hardly any cars passing. This is Vermont.

Isis Notes

Isis-Osiris

lamb, ram, lion, lily, bee
Moses

voyage of soul after death—priests
Amon-Re
Egypt Book of Dead

trials by fire, water, sex

Sphinx—"I am doubt."

winged beast
head of woman, paws of lion

body torn to shreds by jealous brother
scattered throughout Egypt

process of collection
making whole

picking up the pieces
Osiris made whole

mummification

from the past to this present

Gun Law

Lying backward on bed in Massachusetts, staring into blue face of the TV—an ad comes on. A "Public Service Announcement." Massachusetts has a new gun law and it seems the public hasn't caught up with it yet. The scene is a courtroom with a white kid facing a white judge—high up on a podium all decked out in black robes, distinguished gray hair, and imposing grimace. The kid is saying: "Your honor, I'm really sorry, I'll never do it again." The judge glares down at him. "The *law* says one year in jail if you're found in the possession of a firearm, young man. There's signs up all over the place to that effect." Now the camera zooms in for a tight shot on the judge's face. He directs the punch line straight to the camera. "Haven't *you* seen them?

Boston

I s Boston all that heavy as the papers make out? Is any place heavy if you're just moving through and out the other side? People seem to believe the topics. The topics create the atmosphere. Even over clam chowder you hear it going on. "Busing," "gun laws," "sex crimes," "murder." Back to back with traditionally powerful intellectual community. The Seat of the Nation. The Underpants is more like it. The Higher Education marketplace. Harvard, Yale, Radcliffe, bookstores up the ass. Bookstores, murder, chain of violent repercussions. Gestapo outfits on cops. Third Reich sirens. Professors. Judges. Law and School. Law School. Law and ORDER! The Chained Animal of the City. Sleepy lobster beach towns. "MONEY DOESN'T TALK IT SCREAMS!" Money oozing out the suburbs. Dylan fits this atmosphere like a super counterspy. A sneak thief in the dead of night. Vanishing like the Lone Ranger. Painted white mask and a mouthful of heart.

Opposite: "Is Boston all that heavy?"

Sloman in the Lobby

Sloman has caught up with us again. I've never quite figured out how he got connected with the tour in the first place. Rumor has it that Dylan hired him personally to write a book on the tour. Articles on the tour keep appearing in *Rolling Stone*, *The Village Voice*, even *The New York Times* with his by-line. Imhoff keeps booting him out of every hotel he shows his face in. Finally at this one (the Sheraton Inn, Foxboro, Massachusetts), Sloman has wigged out from what he terms "maltreatment." He's storming around the lobby in a coonskin Davy Crockett cap, his usual tennis shoes, and a Hurricane Carter T-shirt, yelling at the top of his lungs. "I'm tired of being jerked off! Everybody's jerking me off! *Rolling Stone*'s jerking me off! Even my girl friend's jerking me off! I'm tired of being a fuckin' Nigger!" This is all going over big with the management, who stand tensely behind the registration desk looking like ticket sellers to a Disneyland sideshow. Dylan is rocking back and forth on his heels, smiling at Sloman. Imhoff is even laughing at him. He asks Sloman what he wants that will make him happy. Sloman goes over the top with his list of demands. He's got them all scribbled down in pencil on a piece of notepaper and begins to run off the list for the benefit of the entire hotel. "I want a per diem! I want passes! I want an I.D. card just like everybody else! How come I don't have an I.D. card? I want access!" Imhoff turns to Dylan. "Shall we put him on the crew bus, Bob? At least that way we can keep an eye on him." Dylan nods. Sloman joins the bus. He starts doing cartwheels through the lobby with his girl friend. If Dylan ever wondered how far a fan would go to get tight with him, he's looking at it in the flesh.

On the Laundry Trail

November 22, Sheraton Inn, Foxboro, Massachusetts

I'm on the trail of my laundry, which is somewhere waiting in a laundry room on the other side of this Sheraton Inn. The journey takes me down through pumpkin-orange halls with chocolate trim around the doors, out into an enclosed dining hall with guests eating, waterfall architecture, piped Musak, up sculptured steps, onto AstroTurf surrounding pool, and back into pumpkin-orange halls on other side. Now the collage of "wild" sound on this particular trip is extraordinary and the notation of it begins from the relatively silent hallway contrasted with the sudden deluge of dining-room noises, rushing water, voices eating, piped sound all happening in a large confined space. Then, again the contrast entering the hallway on the other end coming to relative silence. I'm inside. Contained again. Closed controlled atmosphere. Constant blowing temperature like Greyhound-bus air. I'm looking for the laundry but in my ears is a cricket. How could a cricket be the dominant sound in closed space? How could a cricket even be in a place like this? The shock of it causes me to go paralyzed on the spot. Just staring down to the end of the corridor. Listening more than looking. From the far end of the hall coming straight for me is a tiny girl in a nightgown with a doll in her hand. It's a real little girl. The combination of this sight along with the solitary cricket is more than I can fathom. The cricket goes on. I've never had anything but the most peaceful associations with crickets. It's one of my all-time-favorite sounds on the planet. It's so powerful to my general psyche, in fact, that it totally transforms this labyrinth of hotel lunacy into a paradise. I'm floating on the sound of a single cricket. The little girl has disappeared but the cricket keeps on. I find a door that swings open to my laundry piled on a straight-back chair. The sight of my own clothes sitting in a foreign cement room with a cricket for a soundtrack, thousands of miles from my home, is almost too much for my general condition. I begin folding my T-shirts, rolling my socks into balls, folding my jeans. I'm humbled beyond belief. I want to pray to this cricket. I want to talk to this cricket somehow, but he's nowhere in sight. I hate leaving this cricket behind.

Bangor, Maine

Maine still looks like a State of innocence. The cops aren't looking crazed. In fact they look more like the last remnants of a formality they have to go along with because all the newspapers claim these things are "potentially explosive situations." Dylan appears with huge white crosses on his cheeks, coming closer and closer to a Sioux medicine man and further and further from *Children of Paradise*. The evolution of his make-up on this tour could take up a whole other book. His hat is growing yellow flowers now with a sprig of pine shaking like a turkey feather from side to side.

This is definitely where the tour makes sense. A communal giving of spirit energy through music. No big promotional scams. No tense preparations for putting the show over the top. Just incredible music received by incredible small audiences who take it all in. It's Thanksgiving to boot. A snowstorm outside is making the inside seem even more on fire. Almost like a ritual. If electric rock and roll has "evolved" to a state of hero worship and blind adulation in some spheres, then Rolling Thunder is the antidote. The Medicine. The Medicine Show with a real, true-life Medicine Man, packing real, truly powerful Medicine of the Spirit. Dylan's not without his fanatics, that's for sure, but his heroism transcends being a faddist phenomenon. He moves into mysticism at the drop of an E-minor chord. Because his very identity is a mystery, he pushes the question of "who" he is into "what" he is. What is this strange, haunted environment he creates on stage, on record, on film, on everything he touches? What world is he drawing from and drawing us all into as a result? It's right there in front of us, but no one can touch it.

York Harbor, Maine

Morning. Knock on Dylan's door. Inside he's on the phone, shirtless, ordering frankincense and myrrh, royal jelly, long distance. We go outside and stare at a picnic table, the harbor behind. A couple lobster boats with Buick flathead engines, going like cats out to sea. He talks about the possibility of discovering America. Right here. Right here at the picnic table. "How 'bout that? We discover America at a picnic! Go get Neuwirth and tell him. It's the perfect weather for it. And try to get a boat for Jack. We'll get Jack in the boat with a captain's hat, and he comes around the point and discovers us at the picnic table." We're off and flying. Many lobsters are ordered. Waitresses are hired on the spot. Lobstermen show up. Within an hour the placid seaside surroundings are humming with movement. Ken, the cameraman with exclusive rights on the tour photos, has six machine-driven cameras hanging off his neck like black weights. All he does is press down and they fire off shots like rounds in a Thompson submachine gun. He's waited eight years for this chance, he says. More food from the kitchen is brought and dumped on the picnic table. Magnums of champagne. One of the lobstermen is watching from the side with his son. Both of them standing in rubber boots and slouched caps watching everyone run around. "Last time they hired me for a cigarette commercial and I waited six days for the right sunset. They were payin' me good but they never did use the boat. I could be out collectin' my traps right now."

It's hard to see the far-reaching effects of a project like this. The power rests in money, in media-enforced stardom, in constant movement with anything and everything accessible. Any need of the moment can be satisfied within minutes. If you need a boat, just go out and buy off a lobsterman. Nothing's outside the realm of possibility.

"He moves into mysticism at the drop of an E-minor chord."

Riptide

The feeling now is that it's ridiculous to talk about what kind of film we're making. The whole thing is a booming event beyond film, beyond tape recorders, beyond any attempt to capture the whole of it. There's no way to even document this thing. It's all happening at once in a million directions. The only thing now is to allow it to unfold in any way it wants and to just run with it. To pace it like you would a racehorse. Give space wherever it's needed. To try to keep watch on it and stay open to its risings and fallings. To stay away from giving vent to hysteria and madness at the lack of form. It's not formless anyway. It's just that most of us are out of touch with the form that it's really taking and feel it sweeping us along like a riptide.

Granada in the Rain

Shelbourne, Vermont—another backwoods resort we pull into after miles of bus and van travel. Local New Englanders seen through the window, dipping lobster tails in butter. Candlelight glowing in the dining room. There's a steady pouring coming down as we wait in the various vehicles for word on our rooms. Turns out the management isn't sure if they have enough rooms for us. They weren't expecting us for another day or so. I spot Sloman lurking around in his big rented red Ford Granada. At this point he's never sure whether Barry has arranged a room for him or if he'll be kicked out into the Holiday Inn circuit. He's trying to be inconspicuous, but in a car like that it's hard to be invisible. I can see that this hanging around is going to take up at least another hour, so I slide out of the bus and maneuver my way over to Sloman and the Ford. I've never been behind the wheel of one of these middle-of-the-road Fords, so I convince Sloman to let me take it out for a spin while we're waiting. He hands me the keys and runs to seek shelter from the downpour. Now this is it. From the second I turn over the ignition I can feel a great lurch of independence surging through me. No more bus, no more van, no more hotel-zoo. I pound down on it and leave a steaming swath of black rubber clear through the parking lot. Out onto the country roads. The car handles like a tiger. A little narrow for making 180-degree sliding turns, but if you forget about having ever driven a Dodge Charger, it's not bad. It's a strange sensation to suddenly find yourself barreling down through a small Vermont town in a rented car with a California driver's license and no particular destination in mind. Just the idea that right now you could head anywhere. North, across the border, into Quebec, Montreal, any old place. It would take them days to track the thing down, and by that time you'd be in Canada. "Then what?" I'm asking as rows of antique shops are zipping past me on all sides. "Then you're in Canada. Then what? How come I feel like escaping? Everything's going all right. I'm not starving. Nobody's oppressing me. What's going on?" I just keep driving, hoping for a local pool hall or even a sandwich shop, but nothing crops up but antique stores. I go flying by them, catching glimpses of wicker rocking chairs, ancient sleighs, mirrors framed in oak, duck decoys, Indian baskets. Tourist haven. Little outlets for boredom. For retired gentry killing off the time that's left them. I go into a drastic fishtail off the side of the road and head up a dirt path designed strictly for walking. The Granada's doing vertical fandangos, trying to keep its suspension in line with the ruts. The path seems to be going nowhere fast. Straight into the woods. Just more rain and a thick mat of maple leaves being pulverized under the wheels. The thought occurs to turn back and at least put the wheels on hard pavement, but for some reason I keep heading straight into it. No houses even. No cows. Just trees. Slowly, this renegade impulse starts to leave me, and the Granada peters out by a small stand of cherry trees. I just leave the lights on and the motor idling and sit there staring out through the windshield. Windshield wipers slapping themselves silly. "Okay, now you've escaped. Now what?" I'm still not getting an answer.

"The band is flying."

Waterville, Maine

Maine is the perfect environment for Rolling Thunder. Everything seems to fit the intentions of the tour here except for the consistently lame hotels we get kenneled into. Once outside these confines though, the real feel of land creeps through and even people who live here come into the picture. A blind guy sits at one end of a bar with Dylan at the other, chugging on brandies. They're introduced very slowly and a truly amazing thing takes place. Here's someone who's not out to penetrate Dylan, who can't even see him, who's never even seen a picture of him but only heard his music over all these years. He stands there looking slightly sidewise over Dylan's shoulder, white eyes with smiling creases at the corners. He's a musician. Dylan's gaze goes into him all the way. They talk about trading cowboy shirts. They talk about seeing and hearing. There's no show of bravado going on because there's one pair of eyes missing. The next night Dylan, from up on stage, dedicates a song to the guy.

The audiences in Maine are strictly country. Big kids who've rushed to the concert from dairy farms, just finished milking, cow shit on their boots, overalls. These are the first towns where the feeling of Dylan's presence being a rare gift is felt for sure. The concert in Augusta taps some special energy field that I haven't seen so far. The band is flying. Dylan playing the instrumentals with his back to the audience in a circle with the other guitars, like an Arapaho rain dance. From high above, in the side bleachers, his mother is watching with the kids. Mrs. Baez is up there too. This is really happening. A family event in the heart of the sticks with the world's original superstar tap-dancing to an audience of farmers' kids. Dylan comes off dripping sweat like a rainstorm. Barry Imhoff is waiting faithfully just off stage with an armload of fresh towels. Dylan kisses his mother on the cheek, grabs a towel, and trots off toward the dressing room, guitar neck pointing to the ground. The place is supercharged. Even the Hurricane benefit at the Garden had nothing on these small halls in the depths of a state that the government officially terms a "depressed area." That is, they got no money.

Pink Dunkin' Donuts

The film-crew truck has reached a point of manic hysteria after four straight hours of road, sharing the inside of a van with all the equipment and running thin on stories of sexual bravado. We brodey into a pink Dunkin' Donuts before finishing off the last eighty-five miles. Our buzzing bodies are met by the sight of two waitresses dressed in straight pink behind a pink counter with pink stools with a pink cash register mounted on chrome. The unending list of donuts of all possible combinations runs from floor to ceiling in various tones of pink—"Maple Bars, Old Fashioned Chocolate Walnut, Coconut Cream, Powdered Lemon, Custard Cream, Raspberry Filled, Apple Turnovers"—until the stomach is doing back flips clear out onto the highway just from the very imaginings of these items hitting the soft palate. A handful of locals are dunking their donuts religiously into pink cups of caramel-colored coffee. Our hysteria is mounting in small leaps, and we seem to be carrying on like a bunch of GIs bopping into Saigon for a little side action. It must be a mixture of fatigue and that strange liberating sensation to know that this place is permanent to some and only temporary to us. In fact it's unreal to think of any place as permanent once movement has taken root as a way of life. We strike up a few words with one of the chubby waitresses and question her about several red welts standing up on her wrists, making a built-in bracelet. She reveals that she came by them from playing "chicken" with cigarette butts. I find myself asking her if she knows the one where you strap a dollar bill to your wrist and try to burn a hole through it with a cigarette. If you get the hole all the way through, you get to keep the dollar. Few make it. She's never tried. I don't have the heart to challenge her. Talk shifts to the possibilities of robbing the pink cash register. She's game for that one but says the manager's already come by and collected all the hard stuff. "I'd do it though," she claims. "I'd do anything to get out of here." "Where would you go?" says us. "Anywhere. I'd go with you guys." We beat a hasty retreat to the van with the vision of her mopping up the donut crumbs in a pink background.

The Last Shaker Village

Barreling through the snow with Jack at the wheel in search of the last of the original Shaker villages. The Shakers are a celibate religious sect notorious for their simplicity in furniture making and mode of life. I'm not sure what the reasons for choosing their village as a potential location were, but all I'm ready for right now is a hot bath and a bed. The car is totally smog-bound with reefer smoke, plastic coffee cups crackling under our feet, old clothes pushed against the back window. None of us has had a shave for a week and we're lost on the back roads. We stop and Mel phones ahead to the top Shaker to let them know we'll be late. It's ten o'clock already and way past their bedtime. We finally locate their houses on a stretch of lonely road. Big beautiful white clapboard masterpieces of early American architecture. They really are something to take in. Especially glistening in white light in the nighttime snow. The Shakers are patiently waiting for us on the front porch. One woman and two men, all slightly over middle age or thereabouts, dressed in very plain clothes but nothing resembling a uniform or religious vestment. Between the three of us we've managed to disappear about eight j's, each the size of a Tiparillo cigar, and our exit from the car must seem a little obvious to the Shaker folks. We manage to forage our way through the bright snowbanks and come to rest on their porch. They're very cordial people and not at all irritated by our late arrival. They welcome us inside to a warm hallway of tongue-in-groove maple paneling. A staircase with a hand-rubbed cherry wood handrail. Everything is totally neat and scrubbed to the bone. Not a trace of dust anywhere and every single article in its place. It's as though just by our going inside we're confronted head-on with the opposite state of being that we find ourselves in. Here it's obvious that everything runs like clockwork. A rigorous schedule to the day's activities. Nothing operates without a plan. And nothing is undertaken but the most practical tasks. We stand there shuffling the snow off our shoulders like three renegade fur trappers while they take us all in. The odd thing is that I feel absolutely no judgment coming from them. They aren't comparing their way of life to ours. They seem not to care about the way we look or the fact that we're obviously zipped out of our minds. We follow the oldest Shaker down the hallway and into an immense kitchen with long tables, "original" handmade chairs and rows of copper kettles hanging from brass hooks. Mel is trying to carry on some semblance of sober rationality with the man while at the same time looking like something out of a Charles Dickens nightmare. "Well, what we'd like to do, if this meets with your approval, is to have Joan and Bob come down with just a few of the others and just sort of look the place over. Just to see if it fits into Bob's idea of the film." The Shaker senior is nodding and smiling and rocking back on his heels as though inwardly laughing his ass off. "That's fine with us. We'd be glad to have them." The woman chimes in that she'd like to fix the stars a special home-cooked Shaker meal in exchange for Joan singing a few of her songs. Slowly this is beginning to feel like the wrong ball park, but we have to go through with the grand tour of the place, feeling morally obliged after being so late. We follow them all upstairs, where more Shakers are sitting around in rocking chairs knitting and working on some kind of craft or other. The oldest Shaker is showing us pictures and portraits of the original people who founded the village. "And this is brother Martin, whom you may have heard of in the outside world. He composed the song ' 'Tis a Gift to Be Simple.' " We nod acknowledgment and try to spur the adventure onward, since hunger is starting to grip us from all sides. Images of a plastic dinner in a good old plastic restaurant in a good old plastic hotel are flooding our field of vision. Still the Shakers march on through the colossal old house, stopping in every nook and cranny to dig out some thimble or needle that was used by one of the "sisters" back in the 1700s somewhere. I suddenly see that this whole thing is a museum. Not just a museum of objects but of an entire way of life that these people are embalming in the flesh. They've all retired from "the life out there in the big mean nasty world" in preference for preserving an idealized morality of the past. Everywhere there seems to be a great starvation for tradition and true culture in this country, and these people seem to have answered that need for themselves by cutting themselves off completely. Rolling Thunder is starving for something too but at the opposite end of the stick. By throwing themselves in completely. By sniffing through the past for pieces of evidence that could lead us to a truer picture of the present. How did we arrive where we are now? What series of events actually went down to cause us to be at this point in time? Where exactly are we? On the road to our dinner in a plastic hotel.

Shaker village.

Dylan Monologue

Film

"I was lookin' for myself in this country store. I was informed. I was told by certain sources that this was the place. I had no idea why. I mean from the outside it looked like any other joint. Firewood for sale, stuff like that. So I went inside and asked if they'd seen me. I just asked straight out like that. They sorta looked at me like I was crazy and told me to wait right there. They disappeared into back rooms and there I was. Just standing there. So my body started moving while I was waiting there. Sorta dancing. Looking around. Kickin' the floor. Tapping. Then I started talking to myself like no one could hear what I was up to. I started listing things around me. Everything the eyes could see and the ears could hear. Making lists to myself. Chain saws, hammers, cheese barrels, cracker barrels, crackers, rednecks, preachers, panthers, nails, jigsaws, horses, hobbyhorses, sawhorses, outboard motors, rain clouds, lightning, lumber trucks, pig meat, breakfast, tea cups, dancers, Nijinsky, divers, deep seas, oceans, rivers, railroad, rapers, radio, waves, mothers, sons in battle, danger, ideas, magic, warlords, ghost bombs, replicas, machine shops, galaxies, torture, treasure hunts, band leaders, Dixieland, wheat crops, tractors, trailers, engineers, bodyguards, cheetahs, Mexico, badlands, desert life, organs, drum rolls, executions, crucifixions, embalmings, ambulances, bloody hands, gimmicks, inventions of the mind, inventions of the body, sporting goods, taxis, rolling pins, ball bearings, working parts, blisters, broken backs, white-face cattle, robber barons, landlords, dressing rooms, diamonds, fast hands, goose bumps, Apaches, dingo dogs, and monkeys in space. And then I just ran out."

Thanksgiving

Holiday Inn

Homesickness is hitting me strong, even though Barry Imhoff has done everything a producer could to turn this snowbound Holiday Inn into a family atmosphere. Great long tables arranged in a horseshoe, complete with white tablecloths and all the holiday trimmings. Dylan's kids kicking dozens of colored balloons past the waitresses' heads as they weave toward the tables balancing steaming golden turkeys and platters of cranberry sauce. It's not exactly "life on the farm," but it fills the gaps left by six weeks of room service and "take-out" hamburgers. Halfway through the main course a pitching contest breaks out between opposing tables, using cashew nuts, turkey leg bones, small white after-dinner mints, and an assortment of side orders. Lou is really getting into it and perfecting high arcing lobs with creamed onions, using a spoon for a catapult. Myers and the rest of "B-Unit" come staggering in from the cold, shaking snow off them like a scene out of *Yukon King*. Most of the turkey's been devoured, and they go back into the kitchen in search of leftovers. The kids have really taken over now, diving under the tables and bombing each other with turkey carcasses. Dylan sits in an overcoat and hat picking over the remains of his giblets. He rarely looks up from his plate, as though anything worth seeing could be just as well heard and felt through the atmosphere. There's a sudden crash from one end of the room and a loud gurgling roar coming from Dave Myers, who's pushed over an entire table, glasses, silverware, plates, the whole shot. He begins pounding both fists on the fallen table, bellowing "FOOD! FOOD!" over and over. Evidently he didn't find any in the kitchen. This is turning into a far cry from what the Pilgrims had in mind. Dylan looks up slowly, eyes toward the chaos, then goes back to his giblets. The waitresses are hauling in cakes, pies, puddings, and stuff like that. B-Unit goes ape shit tearing into the rich goodies. Dylan's mother is helping herself to seconds and seems to be enjoying life on the road. The accountant brings by a stack of veterinary certificates for the dogs, in order for them to cross the Canadian border. Everything seems to be in order. This is the last night on the tour for me. In the morning I head for the Big Apple by rent-a-car while Rolling Thunder crosses over into Quebec and places north. I'm getting a little nervous about my suitcase. Peter Orlovsky seems to have forgotten which bus he's packed it into. I round up Peter and his ponytail and we head out into the snow in search of the buses. Peter has a huge ring of keys which he jangles, as though by jangling in a certain order the right key will magically appear between his fingers. The blizzard is hitting us in the face like a Marlboro commercial, and even with insulated boots the freezing wet stuff gets through to the skin. Each bus has about four huge luggage compartments and each compartment has a different key. The whole thing is turning into a Zen koan with a "beat poet" at the helm, shuffling through each key in the dark, in a blizzard, in the middle of Maine with an insane dinner party only fifty yards away, with the bus leaving the country in a few hours, with my suitcase buried under miles of sound equipment, and with me left in a Holiday Inn. There's nothing all that valuable in the suitcase; it's just the idea of us going our separate ways after having traveled together so long. Me and the suitcase, that is. Peter finally surfaces with what he thinks is the right key, and presto the long corrugated metal door rises like a southern California garage. Peter starts hauling all the baggage out one piece at a time into the snow. The cavern grows deeper and darker but still no sign of my suitcase. He flips his ponytail over his left shoulder, makes an "I can't figure it out" noise, and starts putting each piece back in. We repeat this process eight times, him handing me the pieces, me setting them in the snow, then me handing them back to him again until finally on the eighth compartment we strike gold. There it is in the deepest corner sitting on its end right next to a guitar case. Peter snorts. "I'll be darned. I was thinkin' we'd probably have to start lookin' in the semi for it."

Night of
the Hurricane

December 9—Madison Square Garden. The Garden is sold out
for the concert within five hours after the box office opens.
The question is, why the Garden after all that talk of keeping the show
on a small-town level? Why wrap it up with a giant fandango in New
York City? It seems like a combination of helping to heal the costs of
money lost on the New England circuit plus a genuine interest in
aiding Rubin Carter. It is billed as a benefit, and it's for sure that the
"public interest" generated by the presence of Muhammad Ali and
Dylan in the same space is going to leak down to that New Jersey
jailhouse and work its own kind of leverage on the law. Already the
papers are talking about reprieves and retrials, and there's no doubt
that this event will add some muscle to the whole cause.

In the afternoon the Garden is totally empty except for a few
janitors and the Neuwirth band doing a sound check. The levels are
generally too high, which seems to be coming from the impulse to put
the music across in this gigantic tomb after playing to so many tiny
halls for weeks on end. Mansfield has a superkeen ear and it doesn't
take long before the vocals match up with the bottom end. I climb my
way up to the very top of the volcanolike auditorium until the band
looks like a miniaturized Punch and Judy show. Nobody's face is
recognizable. Only certain random gestures give any clues as to who
they are. It's very strange to know these people and then see them
from the audience's point of view. The Garden is a stupefying piece of
suspended architecture. Not beautiful or even aesthetic, but you can't
help but wonder how they came up with a design for this gargantuan
ceiling that seems to be just hanging in midair. No pillars or columns
anywhere. Just cables all coming into a central hub and somehow
holding the whole thing up. Seeing it with only a few people in it
really adds to the immensity of it. I keep moving around to different
places in the auditorium and sitting for a few minutes in each place
just to see what it's like. I begin to notice certain sections filling up
with people. In one section all the people are wearing blue. In another
section, white. Then a whole section of brown people. I start
descending the mountain to take a closer look at this phenomenon. It
turns out that the blue people are cops. All of them sitting within a
definite perimeter, sucking on coffee cups, jackets open, feet up on
the backs of chairs, and talking to each other. The brown people are
ushers, doing more or less the same thing as the cops and carrying

flashlights. The white people are technicians. Each section totally cut off from the other section like little territories on a topographical map. There's something very warming to me about all this, but I can't figure out what it is.

I make my way backstage, imagining all the different atmospheres this place has contained and how amazing it is that it still remains without a physical identity of its own. It's just a building and then a whole world enters into it and takes it over and then goes away again. Dog shows, rodeos, circuses, prizefights, hockey games, basketball, horse shows, ballets, musical events. The smell of hot roasted chestnuts and sauerkraut brings me out of my stupor. Barry Imhoff has done it again. He's hired a hot-dog man and a pretzel man from off the street, and they're both handing out their steaming stuff to anyone who wants it. It's been a while since I've had a real New York hot dog with mustard and sauerkraut and onions, so I stop. As I'm standing there waiting for the little fat man to pile all these layers onto two white buns resting in a piece of cellophane, I notice what seems to be a small army of black men in pinstripe suits, grim-set faces, eyes darting in all directions, all swarming around an even bigger, taller black man dressed completely in black and looking a lot like the "heavyweight champeen of the whole entire world." My two hands go paralyzed, one reaching in my pocket for change and the other one reaching for the hot dog as my eyes try to shake loose from this vision. Ali is cool and graceful while all around him these other guys never stop rotating their heads and twitching their pockets. If there aren't any assassins around, it looks like they'd just as soon dream one up right there on the spot just to let somebody know they're not fooling around. They move off down the hallway like a colony of worker ants surrounding the queen. The little fat hot-dog man is making "fed up" noises in a New York accent. I pay up and stagger off toward the dressing rooms. This must be the American way all right. Nothing's important or has any value until it's blown up into "bigger than life" proportions. "Get the biggest damn fucking hall in the whole entire planet! Get the heavyweight champ of the whole entire world! Get the greatest folksinger since Edith Piaf! The most incredible poet-musician phenomenon the world has ever seen and throw 'em all together in front of the biggest goddamn flesh-and-blood toe-tappin' audience this side of the Rio Grande! And we'll have ourselves a show, folks!" I'm game.

I veer into a dressing room marked GUAM and come to rest on a metal bench. The table in the middle of the room looks like it couldn't support any more flowers and nuts and fruit. Barrels full of cans of beer, soft drinks resting on ice in every corner. Telegrams from all over pinned to the walls. Ginsberg comes bouncing in wearing a suit and tie plus his youthful tennis shoes. It's a good feeling seeing him in this atmosphere. Like a little breeze of sanity blowing through the door. "My father's out there. He's eighty years old and he's never

seen a rock concert." I ask Allen if he's not afraid his father might have a heart attack at that age. "Naw, my father's a poet." He laughs and goes off bopping into the men's room. He shouts out of the bathroom to me. "He is! A real poet! We gave a reading together the other day at a college up north!" Neuwirth joins us, spinning on both heels, nervous as a cat. Already he's worked himself up into a lather. He growls something unintelligible, cranes his neck as though looking for someone, and then pivots back out the door. Most everyone is catching this drift of emotional frenzy. I can't remember the feeling of tension being like this at any other time on the tour except for maybe the very first concert at Plymouth. But that was mostly just butterflies, hoping the show would get off the ground on an up note. But this is more verging on anxiety. To add to it, Roberta Flack has been called in at the last minute because Aretha Franklin was tied up with dates in Los Angeles. Roberta makes no bones about being picked as second string to the great Aretha. She comes on like full-tilt Hollywood, storming around backstage in a flashy bandanna, decked out in jewelry and shouting orders to her entourage. There's a definite taste of black-white tension going on backstage, which is another new ingredient that was lacking on the New England schedule. Nothing weird or violent, just these two totally different streams of musical culture swimming by each other without mixing. Almost as though there were two different concerts to be given on the same bill, having nothing in common. I keep coming back to the idea that it's a black man that the concert's being given for. A benefit for a black convict initiated by a white singer with black support. It's too sticky to figure out. Ali's been trying to trump up support for Carter for quite a while. Before Dylan even. But it took Dylan to get this whole thing together.

Back in the auditorium the audience is steadily sifting in, filling up the entire cavern like salt in an egg timer. Lola, an old friend of the tour who left somewhere up in Vermont, is back tonight for the big one. She's broken a heel off her boot and has a cop doubled in half trying to hammer it back on with the handle of his gun. Someone else donates some epoxy and a popsicle stick. Pretty soon three or four people are crowded around Lola and the broken boot, adding their two cents' worth. None of the repair methods seems to be working, and she's getting more and more anxious as the time for the first set to open draws nearer. The idea of her hobbling around the whole night on one broken boot, otherwise dressed to the nines, has her on the verge of hysteria. I offer to run backstage and see if I can borrow a spare boot off one of the women in the tour. Joni Mitchell has only one pair and she's not parting with them, since she's going on stage in about ten minutes. Ronee Blakely is wearing a pair of black high-heeled English jobs which she warns me are her very favorite boots, hand tailored to fit her extra-small foot. She agrees to loan them if I swear on a stack of bibles to get them back to her before the night's over. I run out of the dressing room with the boots flapping in front of me, feeling like a surrealistic decathlon runner. I wedge my way through to Lola, who's now surrounded by "repairmen," and present her with the fancy boots. She stabs her foot down into one of them, full of hope that she's found the solution, only to come to a crunching dead end at the ankle. Still full of determination she goes on cramming and yanking until a low ripping, popping-of-stitches sound begins to emerge from the boot. I don't have the heart to tell her to stop, but she finally has to, since there's no way her American foot is going to conform to English style. She heaves a sigh of despair and then tries to back her way out, but since her first efforts were so forceful, the boot is now frozen solid in a halfway position that looks like it could become worse than having no boots at all. Now the men come back into the picture. Each one grabbing the heel and hoisting backward as Lola clings to the railing, grimacing as though the whole process were worse than labor pains. Now the cop takes a turn and even unbuttons his blue jacket for the attempt. Finally the boot is born with a mighty ripping of the calfskin, and the entire inner lining is left hanging in shreds. Lola is lying in a heap on the floor gasping for air as I grab the boot before it can come to any more disaster and dash off for the dressing room again. My head is going through all kinds of contortions trying to figure out the right way to present the mishap to Ronee. All the time I'm stuffing the lining back inside the boot, hoping it will somehow glue itself back together again. The dressing room's empty except for T-Bone, who says that Ronee's decided to go on in tennis shoes, since her best boots are being "borrowed" for the night. I'm standing there like a shoplifter caught in the act and decide the best place for the boots is behind a pile of towels in a darkened corner. I can always put the explanation off till later. I sprint back to the arena.

The whole atmosphere has changed now with the coming of the crowds. Even the air is different. New York really is the testing ground for any experiment. It's plain as day. If you want the world to know about it, bring it to New York. Better yet, bring it to the GARDEN!

The band kicks off into "Good Love Is Hard to Find" and the volcano erupts. Rolling Thunder meets itself head-on in the voice of over thirty-five hundred screaming beings from earth. Dylan may be just a kid from Minnesota but this here is his hometown. No matter how many politico-music critics find disappointment in his recent lyrics and his life style, the people here tonight are saying YES in full strength. Bring on the punk who changed the entire face of American youth consciousness in one fell swoop! Generally the musicians seem to be pushing themselves to the point where the music seems strained and speeded up compared to the more informal concerts up north. Ronson, on the other hand, really gets off on this monster crowd. His initial style is broad and theatrical anyway, coming from English "rave-up" and David Bowie. He begins to uncork all the flash he's been holding back throughout the tour. Giant, spread-eagle leaps into thin air. Triple vertical spins, wrapping the guitar cord around him like a boa constrictor, slashing at the guitar with huge full-arm uppercuts. Platinum-blond hair spraying in all directions. Then stalking around the stage, stiff legged, Frankenstein macho strutting, shaking the neck of the guitar with his vicious chord hand as though throttling his weaker brother. All the time, never losing a lick. Through every motion playing genius, inspirational lead lines, then melting into the background again to support the other musicians. Neuwirth seems on the verge of exploding through his skin from sheer tension. His voice is splitting down the middle through every song. The band holds it together though. Right down the line it's the music that's making this whole thing happen. The solid experience behind every member of the band. Joni Mitchell blows the top off the place again, just by walking on. She looks incredibly small from where I'm sitting. Like a vulnerable little girl trying to sing a song she's written for a huge living room full of adults. One of Neuwirth's standard introduction lines at every concert has been, "Welcome to your living room," and tonight's the first night I've really seen what he means. The set rolls on and then Muhammad Ali is introduced. This is becoming like a study in emotional trauma. It's hard to believe how the space can contain any more hysteria than it's already had, but Ali is like nitroglycerin wherever he appears and tonight is no exception. He cools the audience down and starts in with one of his casual lines that make you feel like he's talking to you personally and not thousands. "You know, when they asked me to come here tonight, I was wondering who this guy Bob Dylan was. Then I show up and see that all these people come to pay money and I think this Bob Dylan must be something. I thought I was the only one who could pack this joint out. Did all you girls really come here tonight to see Bob Dylan?" Huge cheer explodes from the house. "All right, all right. He ain't as purty as me though, you'll have to admit. Now I just want to say that it's a pleasure to see such a turnout here tonight, especially when it's for the cause of helping a black man in jail. 'Cause everyone knows that you got the complexion and the connections to get the protection." Now here comes the real theatrics. One of Ali's aides walks out onto the stage carrying a telephone. Someone interrupts him at the microphone and whispers in his ear. The whole thing's been planned long in advance but it's being put across like it's just now happening. Ali pulls back from the man and grabs the microphone. "I've just been told that we have a special phone call right here that's been put through all the way from New Jersey by special order from the governor. We've got Mr. Rubin 'Hurricane' Carter on the phone and you're going to be able to hear his voice as he's speaking to me." Ali picks up the phone and Carter's voice can be heard as though it's coming through thousands of miles of submerged cable. It sounds much farther away than New Jersey but comes across totally clear-headed and eloquent. In fact, Hurricane Carter sounds more present just through his voice than most of the flesh-and-blood people here. The whole reality of his imprisonment and our freedom comes through loud and clear. "I'm sitting here in jail and I'm thinking that this is truly a revolutionary act when so many people in the outside world can come together for someone in jail." Ali is still aware of the audience and tries to lighten it. "Listen, Rubin, just promise me one thing. If you get out, just don't come and challenge me for the title, all right?" Rubin keeps on, not having to pay dues to an audience he's not even in front of. "On a more serious note, I'm speaking from deep down in the bowels of a New Jersey peniten-tiary." The dialogue keeps on and the audience is surprisingly intent on listening to Carter even with the anticipation of Dylan still in the cards. The solitary voice keeps sailing into every corner of the place like a phantom. The imagination is working double time conjuring up images of this man, locked up and speaking over a phone somewhere to an audience he can't even see. The phone call ends and Ali spins into his next piece of histrionics. "Now. ladies and gentlemen, I'd like to introduce to you tonight the next President of the United States." What's going on now? Nobody's prepared for this one. Dylan's backstage ready to go on for the second half of the show and Ali's up there pulling off a sleeper on everyone. "Now, you know that I'm known for making predictions. And if it hadn't been for this man getting me his own private plane at the very last minute, I couldn't have been here with you tonight." Ali leaves to the sound of massive booing as his white "candidate" appears from out of nowhere, looking like a cross between Howard Hughes and ex-mayor Lindsay. The booing keeps up and rises in volume and intensity as the man tries to speak a few words on his own behalf. It's a pathetic demonstration of bad timing and totally out in left field in terms of what the whole concert and tour has been about. The "next President of the United States" gets about three words in underneath the mounting din of disapproval, then slinks sheepishly off stage. By this time every-body's champing at the bit for Dylan. As usual he just appears. Nobody announces him, he simply sidles out there with his head slightly down, plumes shaking, white-face thicker than usual, and starts singing. He's always got the jump on the audience that way. He knows he's out there way before they do, and it gives him the edge every time. Now the place is storming again. He's rocking back on both heels, doing a duet with Neuwirth on "My Masterpiece." Wyeth's jackhammer drums are splitting the four-four time into smithereens. He has a right hand that's not to be believed. It comes down on the accent and then plays half a dozen little cluster strokes in between striking two or three cymbals for added color. A drummer like this usually goes totally unnoticed, since he lacks the obvious flash of the more athletic types who leap around the set using twice as

"It's a good feeling seeing [Allen] in this atmosphere."

many muscles as they need to. Howie sits there like he's driving a '58 Impala, cruising down the highway while his arms and legs follow the patterns with the minimum of effort.

Halfway through the set Baez has worked out a "groupie" routine where she dashes on stage in blue hot pants, blond wig, and high heels. The security guards go along with the gag and drag her off stage kicking and howling. Later, she pulls off a real show stopper by coming on dressed completely as Dylan. For a second you think you're seeing double for sure until she tries to sing like him. Then the whole thing dissolves. It's like an apparition up there. Both of them the same height, dark eyes peering out through white-moon make-up. The same straight-brimmed hat, black vests. There's so many mixtures of imagery coming out, like French clowns, like medicine show, like minstrels, like voodoo, that your eyes stay completely hooked and you almost forget the music is going on all this time. Down by the side of the stage, one of the cops is asking me which one is Dylan. I point to him up on stage. "You mean that guy with the funny hat? I was just talking to him!" He jabs one of his sidekick cops with his elbow. "Hey, I was just talking to Bob Dylan! I didn't even know it was him." His sidekick tells him to pipe down and listen to the music. Even the cops are tapping their blackjacks to the band now. The whole joint is like one huge humming organism. I thought I left this whole thing behind up in the far north of Maine, but here I am. No way to walk out on this one. No way for anyone to deny the power of this event.

Back in the dressing room Dylan rushes in ripping the harmonica brace off his neck, make-up dripping in long streams, red eyes popping out. "Rubin's been acquitted! He'll be out by Christmas!" I'm the only one there and I don't know what to say. We just stare at each other. I wish I had something to say back to him but I can't find a thing. Nothing comes out. He turns and darts back out the door.

Opposite: Howie Wyeth.

Following page: Dylan and Ali.

In the Bowels of
the Garden

Steam-breathing tacos are strung out in a line fifty feet long, with all the Mexican trimmings. Huge, cargo-elevator loads of party people are unloaded in what's known as The Felt Forum (named after Mr. Felt, not the fabric). Dylan is moving in slow motion through a coagulated mass of parasites, pulling on his coat like he was Lindbergh just returning. His gray caballero cowboy hat with the dancing plumes is the only thing visible of him. Once in a while a rare snatch of red coat with pink hands clawing it. Movie stars are here, spitting up beer in the aisles in fits of hysterical glee. The place is on fire with unchained energy. Somehow we escape and dive into his camper in a garage situation. An underground garage. Dylan's definitely an escape artist. I've never seen the like of it. He vanishes. Just like that. Now he's at the wheel of this thing, which on the inside, if you didn't see the driver and the steering wheel, could pass for a California ashram. It's dark in this garage, but you can still make out the wide-brimmed hat at the wheel. Several other heads are crowding up the floor space. All silent. I'm taking a leak in the portable bathroom and hanging halfway out in order to see where we're going. As though that could verify the situation somehow. The back is full of fancy women sitting on a thick bed, rolling black joints. The mobile home is moving but we're still surrounded by black space. It lurches like one of those old potato boxcars which were never successfully shock absorbed. I can't believe he's actually driving this contraption after just completing a full four hours of ripsnorting musical magic. Even if the evening was somewhat marred by the political presence of Muhammad Ali's Presidential candidate and the backstage show-biz gyrations of Roberta Flack and company, the Garden was definitely the culmination of something for Rolling Thunder. Now we're hitting the streets and he's starting to crank this monster up to around fifty, which is really hauling ass for an apartment on wheels. Blue clouds of reefer smoke are blinding the windows but you can still catch the outside life. I'm losing track of time and space but it seems we're hitting midtown through some miracle of navigation. He brakes the sucker and bails out in the middle of the road. Now here's the situation. Every one of us inside this hulk of a machine is just along for the ride. Dylan's gone again and it's only us. Just like it was before we got on. The streets are cold, and the vast difference between the womb on wheels and this hard cement is enough to send an honest man backpacking for Montana. The fervor's on us all though and we go in search of the action. Down into an Italian underground restaurant with security guards firmly planted at the door. Gary, the bookie, is frisking everyone with his eyeballs. In a flash he's got their number. He sorts out the goodies from the baddies like an experienced assembly-line technician. Nothing gets past him. If anything tries, he's got several combinations of kidney and tenderloin shots that are guaranteed to leave a dent in your memory. I once made the mistake of putting on gloves with him at a Howard Johnson's while allowing him to remain bare-fisted. I got out of that one with a blue welt on the rib cage the size of a mature jellyfish. Inside, the place looks like it's strictly set up for pizza and wine and no more. The juke box is cranked up full on a Hank Snow medley. At least it feels like that. It feels like it's snowing in my brain. There's an upstairs part to this too which is even darker and slightly more sticky with relationships. Somebody's wife is screaming and Ronson is being pulled into the men's head by two teen-age jewels. This is the life. I descend to the ground floor again. I'm not sure what I'm feeling. This is supposed to mark the end of something. This night. The last gathering of all these people after all that tightly packed time of travel. It doesn't seem like it's over though. Just hitting its stride.

"Rubin Carter
Freed on Bail"

"**P**ATERSON, N.J. (U.P.I.)—Nine years after they were convicted of a triple murder they say they did not commit, former middleweight boxer Rubin 'Hurricane' Carter and John Artis were freed on bail yesterday.

"Bail—$20,000 for Carter and $15,000 for Artis—was posted by the Carter-Artis National Defense Fund.

"During the bail proceedings, Carter and Artis were accompanied by heavyweight champion Muhammad Ali, who along with singers Bob Dylan and Joan Baez have led the movement to free them.

"Wednesday, the New Jersey Supreme Court granted them new trials, citing prosecution promises of leniency against Bradley and Bello, who are suspected of a burglary at the time of the murder."

San Francisco Examiner, March 21, 1976

"Geography of a Horse Dreamer"

New York

Tonight I've got a play opening called *Geography of a Horse Dreamer* at the Manhattan Theatre Club. It's one of those modest off-Broadway jobs that house about ninety. Dylan and Sara want to come, so I'm waiting in the hotel lobby for the Cadillac convertible to haul us all over to the theater. The big boxcar camper pulls up outside and Dylan hops out. My stomach does a full gainer as I see him approaching the hotel. The idea of him sitting in the audience is more like a nightmare than a blessing. He comes through the revolving doors and then starts wandering around the lobby reading all the little plaques on the walls about "what to do in case of fire," the breakfast menu for room service, and directions to the elevators. He pauses at one of these signs long enough for me to scuttle past him out into the street and hail a cab. It's bad enough knowing that he'll be there without having to ride there with him in the same car.

Once at the theater I learn that tonight is strictly for the press, and all the critics are chugging away on martinis in the bar. Great, an audience full of critics and Bob Dylan. Couldn't be worse. It's impossible to escape that feeling of Judgment Day that always accompanies any opening night, but this is getting a little thicker than usual. I start chain-drinking brandies, hoping for some kind of numbing of the nerve endings. A girl I haven't seen in six years comes up to me full of nostalgia. This is worse than holding a full house against a possible four aces. On top of all this, the so-called curtain is being held for Dylan's late arrival. He shows up plastered, along with Neuwirth, Kemp, Sara, and Gary Shafner. They take up an entire row. The play begins and there's a deadly silence throughout the house. It's not intended to be a Greek tragedy, but with newspapermen you can never tell exactly what their approach is going to be. In this case, it's "cadaver city." Not a sound in the whole joint. Just the actors knocking themselves out, hoping for some sign of breathing life out there in the darkness. Dylan starts to twitch as though somebody's given him a bum steer about this whole theater trip he's finding himself in the midst of. I'm standing in the back between the aisles of seats, hoping for an earthquake or some other "act of God" to bring the whole thing to an abrupt close, but nothing happens. Just the same aching silence in the air. I've got nothing against silence, but this is the wrong kind.

I shoot out the back door into a big darkened room with only a piano in it. I can still hear the actors pushing the words of the play as though it were a broken-down freight train about to cut loose any second. Still not a sound from the audience. I'm cringing in the dark. "Why'd he have to come to see this play? Why couldn't he have come to see one of the other ones? One of the ones with music in it or something. One of the ones where the audience laughs!" I'm halfway on the verge of just cutting out all together when Jacques Levy, who directed the play, comes sauntering in like a bear holding out a burning stick of reefer, with a Burt Lancaster grin on his face. "Here's something for the pain, Sam." I bite down on the joint with a vengeance. Everything in me is wondering about the reason for ever wanting to set a word down on paper. If this is the real truth of it, why bother? Why go to all the trouble of getting people to come and pay good money to sit and watch something that doesn't even get them off? Then my head shifts to the idea that they're all critics. Seasoned veterans bored out of their minds by anything that doesn't set fire to their seats. That doesn't work either. Somehow I have to just stand here and face this whole agony of it being a public event. Something you do completely in private is suddenly revealed. It's standing out there in the open, and every aspect of it is glaring out at you in a way it never does in the typewriter. You see it for what it actually is, and not the way you imagined.

The act break comes and I skirmish the staircase down to the bar with the realization that I'm stoned out of my skull. The journey downstairs seems to take four hours, and by the time I reach the bar the whole place is jammed to the gills with the audience. I can't figure out how they got there ahead of me. And now that they're there I don't feel much like going into it, so I hang a U-turn and start back up the stairs. Somehow, in all this, I become convinced that Dylan has left the theater. I don't feel him around anywhere and it doesn't seem likely that he'd sit through something that's wasting his time. He went to a Piñero play the other night and left in the middle of it, so why shouldn't he leave mine? I'm trying to slow my head down enough to at least reach the top of the stairs in one piece.

Now the audience is filing back in for the second act. I feel like I've been ambushed into a time warp. "The intermission's over already? I've just made it to the top of the stairs!" I watch the sullen faces plodding back in for another hour of torture. It looks like a documentary on experimental lobotomy. No Dylan. I don't see him anywhere. Now I'm certain he's done another one of his miraculous vanishing acts. Dissolved without a sign. I try to soothe myself. "It's okay. I can take it. This is good for me. I can take it. It's good for me to taste defeat." Then I see him appear from the bathroom. He throws the door open like a saloon scene from *High Noon*, stuffing a bottle of hooch in one pocket while he fumbles with some notepaper. He's been scribbling notes throughout the play, borrowing pencils from people in the row in front of him. Now it looks like he's trying to file them in some kind of mysterious order in all the pockets of his coat. He keeps shifting the notes to different pockets and weaving toward the door to the theater. He sees me standing there and pauses as though trying to bring certain thoughts into focus. "Hey, Sam, what happens to this guy in the play anyway? Does he ever escape?" I'm dumbfounded for a reply but come out with something like, "That's the reason for seeing the second act." He stares at the floor, his knees shifting slightly as though he's about to go into a nose dive.

"Hey, how come you named that horse in the play Sara D?"

"That's the name of a racing dog in England." It suddenly cuts through me that it's also the name of his wife.

"I mean it's the name of a greyhound. A real greyhound. You know, the kind that race around the track."

He smiles and shuffles through the door, almost making a left turn into the light booth. I don't know what to do with myself. I don't particularly want to hit the streets in this state of mind and I sure don't feel like venturing inside for the second-act horrors. I head for the piano room again.

The silence of the second act is even more penetrating than the first. I last about ten minutes in the dark room before I'm back inside the theater staring at the rows of critics. Two of the "heavies" from the major papers are sound asleep, nodding out over their overcoats folded neatly on their laps. The ones who have managed to stay conscious are peering intently at the play as though it was one of those cut-away bottles showing how ants make their tunnels. At this point in the play the main character is about to get shot up with a hypodermic syringe by a fat doctor. Dylan stands in the back row. "Wait a minute!" Who's he yelling to? The actors? "Wait a second! Why's he get the shot? He shouldn't get the shot! The other guy should get it! Give it to the other guy!" Lou Kemp is trying to haul him back down to his seat. The sleeping critics are snorting in the midst of their dreams. Something is merging into their comatose condition. Dylan is struggling to free himself from Kemp's hammer-lock grip. Neuwirth is telling him to shut up. Finally something is happening! The actors are soldiering on with their parts as though nothing has changed. Finally the Sam Peckinpah sequence begins, with shotguns and catsup all over the stage. Dylan leaps up again. "I DON'T HAVE TO WATCH THIS! I DIDN'T COME HERE TO WATCH THIS!" Lou grabs him again by the bottom of his coat and almost pulls him backward clean off the platform of seats. Sara pays no attention. She sits very regally and cool, looking straight ahead. Dylan is fighting like a cat now to get free as Gary, Lou, and Neuwirth are all trying to hold him to the seat. It's a perfect ending. An explosion in the audience to match the one on stage. Shotgun wadding, bursting blood, and Dylan over the edge. "HE'S NOT SUPPOSED TO GET THE SHOT! THE OTHER GUY'S SUPPOSED TO GET IT!" I look back over to the rows of critics. Suddenly they've come to life, all of them desperately clicking their ball-point pens and scribbling in the dark like crazy. The play comes to an end and Dylan is hurtling over the aisles, looking for the exit. The critics don't know what to make of it. Have they missed something? Who was that masked man that just flew by them in a red coat and a gaucho hat, yelling at the top of his lungs? Is the play over already?